on screen ...

Doctor Who:
the David Tennant years

an episode guide

Jamie Hailstone

SONIC**BOND**

sonicbondpublishing.com

Sonicbond Publishing Limited
www.sonicbondpublishing.co.uk
Email: info@sonicbondpublishing.co.uk

First Published in the United Kingdom 2020
First Published in the United States 2020

British Library Cataloguing in Publication Data:
A Catalogue record for this book is available from the British Library

Typeset in ITC Garamond & ITC Avant Garde
Printed and bound in England

Graphic design and typesetting: Full Moon Media

on screen ...

Doctor Who:
the David Tennant years

an episode guide

Jamie Hailstone

sonicbondpublishing.com

Acknowledgements

As I am often reminded, life is a team sport and this book would not have happened without the support, friendship and kindness of others. So, I will take the opportunity to thank the individuals:

Firstly, the brilliant and wonderful Jennie Ward, who has had to endure months of me blathering about Doctor Who while I wrote this book and has also been dragged around countless filming locations as well. She is one in a million and I couldn't have done this without her.

Dr Robin Bunce of Homerton College, Cambridge. As well as being a former housemate and friend for more than 25 years, Dr Bunce is also Cambridge University's expert on the Daleks. If you ever have a burning question about them, he is your man.

Jonathan Werran, James Evison and Dominic Browne, who are three of the finest fellows you could ever hope to sit in a pub with. Let's hit the Cask Pub and Kitchen in Pimlico soon for a celebratory drink, chaps!

Andrew and Sarah Cooper for being my eyes and ears in Cardiff. We'll do lunch soon.

Christopher Samuel Stone at Longscarf Publications for letting me write several Professor Howe novels. For those of you that don't know, the novels are parodies of well-known Doctor Who stories and help raise money for Children in Need. If you thought the jokes in this book are bad, please check out Professor Howe and the Plastic Peril, Shanghaied Scientists and Crafty Count.

Sam Clayden for taking the picture of me on the back cover.

John and Jussy Mclean, Andrew Diamond, Thomas Barrett at Air Quality News, Andy Lees and David Harrison at Spacehouse, Sophie Service, Michael Burton, Heather Jameson, Dan Peters, Matt Hobley, Tom Hogarth and Jermaine Ivey at Hemming, MJ alumni Chris Smith, Mark Conrad and Paul Marinko, Rhiannon Rees, Liz Cooley, Ed Petrie, Big Boy Bloater, Clive Price, George Luke, Ed Hawkins, Tom Fenwick, Martin Leggatt, Brad Brooks, Jon Thatcher, Flix Gillett and the finest writer I know, Simon Parkin.

Much of the information for this book was gleaned from the pages of *Doctor Who Magazine* and *Doctor Who: The Complete History*. If you want to know even more about the Tenth Doctor, you know where to go.

Stephen Lambe at Sonicbond Publishing for allowing me to write this book, and Andrew Wild for suggesting it in the first place. Basically, it's all his fault.

Finally, the staff at the Brewhouse Project in Arundel, West Sussex, who have kept me fed and watered while I bashed out the last 128 pages.

Apologies to anyone that I've forgotten or missed out. Your name will be in the next one. I promise. Unless I forget, of course. Now, where was I? Oh yes, Barcelona. Allons-y!

on screen ...

Doctor Who:
the David Tennant years

Introduction

Oh, new teeth. That's weird. So, where was I? Oh, that's right! David Tennant, better known to millions of science fiction fans around the world as the Tenth Doctor. For many, he was the greatest incarnation of the Time Lord to have ever graced our television screens. When the Tenth Doctor first appeared at the end of 'Parting of the Ways' on 18 June 2005, the rebooted *Doctor Who* under the stewardship of showrunner Russell T. Davies, executive producer Julie Gardner and producer Phil Collinson was already a ratings winner, but that was nothing compared to was about to follow.

Armed with nothing more than a pinstripe suit, some plimsolls and his trusty sonic screwdriver, the Tenth Doctor took the world by storm. After decades of relative obscurity, *Doctor Who* was sexy. The Doctor had always been smart and heroic, but now he had the added bonus of being boyfriend material. Perhaps, not surprisingly, Tennant quickly won over a whole legion of fans with his geek-chic brand of cool.

As he admitted on BBC Radio 4's *Desert Island Discs* in December 2009:

> To an extent, I was doing it for my eight-year-old self, who had loved the show and grown up as a huge, avid fan. I felt the responsibility not to break it. I feel very proud and relieved that it did not go wrong on my watch.

Born David John McDonald on 18 April 1971, he was a devoted Doctor Who fan from an early age and over the years, he frequently credited the programme as the reason why he wanted to become an actor. Aged eight, he queued up to meet his hero, the Fourth Doctor, Tom Baker at a book signing at John Menzies in Glasgow. As Tennant said, again on *Desert Island Discs:*

> I waited in line and he signed my book. I asked him about his scarf because I was wearing a scarf that my granny had knitted me. He came up with some suitably surreal answer. It was a very important life moment for little me.

At the age of 16, he passed the entry audition at the Royal Scottish Academy of Music and Drama in Glasgow and started studying the following year. After discovering there was already another David MacDonald on the books of the actor's union Equity, he took the surname Tennant in honour of the Pet Shop Boys' frontman, Neil Tennant. After graduating in 1991, the young actor's first job was a touring production of the Brecht play *The Resistible Rise of Arturo Us*. As his professional reputation grew, Tennant was also able to indulge his love of Doctor Who thanks to Big Finish Productions, who since 1999 have held the licence to produce official audio adventures based on the programme.

Tennant's first appearance for Big Finish was playing Nazi guard Feldwebel Kurtzin the 2001 drama Colditz, which starred Sylvester McCoy as the Seventh Doctor. In 2003, he played Colonel Brimmicombe-Wood in the Big Finish adventure Sympathy for the Devil, which starred David Warner as an alternative Doctor. And in 2004, he joined the third series of Big Finish's Dalek Empire series as Galanar, and in the same year, he appeared as Daft Jamie in the Sixth Doctor audio adventure 'Medicinal Purposes', alongside Colin Baker and special guest Leslie Phillips. Tennant also managed to bag a small uncredited part as the caretaker in the 2003 online Doctor Who adventure 'Scream of the Shalka', after discovering it was being recorded in the studio next door to where he was working on Terry Pratchett's The Amazing Maurice and his Educated Rodents.

But it was the title role in the 2005 BBC Three drama Casanova, which would bring Tennant to a wider audience and a shot at playing the role of which he had always dreamed.

As Tennant told a convention audience at Madison Wizard World in Wisconsin USA in April 2016:

> So, I was doing Casanova, and it was written by Russell T. Davies, who at the same time was in the middle of putting together the reboot of Doctor Who, along with Julie Gardner, the executive producer also of both shows. Casanova ended up being my kind of audition for Doctor Who, although I was completely unaware of it at the time, because I didn't know they were looking for anyone. Russell asked me round to his house in Manchester, because he had a couple of rough cuts of the first series of Doctor Who and he knew that I was a bit of a fan and that I might want to see how the show was looking. And then they told me that they wanted me to take over!

At this point, the rebooted show had not even been transmitted. On 31 March 2005, just five days after the first episode *Rose* was broadcast, the news broke that Christopher Eccleston would be leaving at the end of the series. According to Tennant, Davies and Garden asked him before the show was broadcast to come and film the last scene for the series finale, 'Parting of the Ways'.

> Which was odd, because the show hadn't been out yet. So, you were thinking, 'what if I film a little bit for the end of episode thirteen, the show doesn't ever go again and I'm the person who played the Doctor for 35 seconds?' I would probably still have got a Big Finish series out of it, so you know.

As it turns out, Tennant did eventually get a Big Finish series for the Tenth Doctor, but perhaps more importantly, his time as the Doctor brought him countless accolades. In December 2006, the readers of *Doctor Who Magazine* voted him their favourite Doctor of all time, beating the ever-popular Tom Baker. In addition, Tennant won the National Television Awards award for Most Popular Actor in 2006 and 2007, and the award for Outstanding Drama Performance in 2008 and 2010. In 2007, a poll conducted by *Radio Times* crowned Tennant's Doctor as the 'coolest character on television'.

Despite countless accolades and impressive viewing figures, there was always the question of how long Tennant would stay in the role that made him a household name. On 29 October 2008, while appearing via satellite link to accept his award for Outstanding Drama Performance at the National Television Awards, Tennant announced that:

When Doctor Who returns in 2020, it won't be with me.

On the same day, the BBC press office confirmed he would be leaving the Tardis for good after filming four special episodes which would be screened in 2009 and early in 2010.

Tennant said, in the official press release:

This show has been so special to me, I don't want to outstay my welcome. I'm still the Doctor all next year but when the time finally comes, I'll be honoured to hand on the best job in the world to the next lucky git – whoever that may be.

On 1 January 2010, with the conclusion of 'The End of Time (Part Two)', Tennant handed the baton over to Matt Smith, the Eleventh Doctor. But as the First Doctor (William Hartnell) once remarked, it was far from being all over. He would return for Doctor Who's 50th anniversary 'The Day of the Doctor' in 2013, and his own Big Finish series too.

More than a decade on, the Tenth Doctor remains as popular as ever. In August 2019, Fathom Events and BBC Studios showed 'The End of Time' on cinema screens across America, complete with a new interview with the man himself, reflecting on his time as the Doctor and the character's enduring popularity. He even joked about returning for the show's 60th anniversary, which will be in 2023. In the 2019 interview, he said:

The question will inevitably come up, but it won't be for me to decide. It would be fun to do. Jodie [Whittaker], Peter [Capaldi] and Matt [Smith] are all mates. It would be wonderful to be on set with them.

Regardless of whether Tennant ever returns to the role on screen or not, his place in the programme's history books is assured. The Tenth Doctor years were a golden era for the show with the most consistently brilliant run of stories since the 1970s. Tennant might have been doing it for his eight-year-old self, who grew up during that era, but he also gave us a hero and countless adventures that fans will never grow tired of. And now, as the Doctor might say:

Allons-y.

Season Two

'The Christmas Invasion'

Original UK airdate: 25 December 2005
Cast: David Tennant as The Doctor, Billie Piper as Rose Tyler, Camille Coduri as Jackie Tyler, Noel Clarke as Mickey Smith, Penelope Wilton as Harriet Jones, Adam Garcia as Alex, Sean Gilder as Sycorax Leader, Chu Omambala as Blake, Anita Briem as Sally, Sian McDowall as Sandra, Paul Anderson as Jason and Cathy Murphy as Mum
Written by Russell T. Davies
Directed by James Hawes
Music by Murray Gold
Produced by Phil Collinson
Filming dates: principal production work ran from 22 July 2005 to 22 August 2005, with extra days on 6/7/8/22 September, 8 October and 3/10 November
Running time: 58 minutes
Original UK viewing figures: 9.8 million

Review

Looking back, the idea of doing a Doctor Who Christmas special seems like such an obvious idea that it's a wonder that nobody had thought of it before. Although, technically speaking, William Hartnell did get there first with an episode called 'Feast of Steven', which was broadcast on Christmas Day 1965 as part of the epic twelve-part serial, 'The Dalek's Master Plan'. It even ends with the First Doctor turning to camera, breaking the fourth wall and raising a glass to wish viewers a happy Christmas. But 'The Christmas Invasion' also saw the proper debut of the Tenth Doctor and kudos must be given to Russell T. Davies for giving David Tennant a properly heroic entrance quite late on in the story. Even in pyjamas and a dressing gown, he is instantly the Doctor. The latest incarnation is full of swagger, rousing speeches and cheeky grins. It's no wonder that millions of viewers instantly took Tennant to their hearts. That's because 'The Christmas Invasion' is a lot of fun. Russell T. Davies does not shy away from the clichés of the season. No bauble was left unturned in a script that contains robot Father Christmases with flame throwers, killer trees and a snow flurry at the end, which turns out to be ash from a blown-up spaceship. It might be Independence Day with a big dollop of tinsel, but as a yuletide adventure for all the family to enjoy, 'The Christmas Invasion' is a worthy addition to the Doctor Who canon.

The Story

It's Christmas Eve, and the Tardis crash lands on the Powell Estate in London. A newly-regenerated Doctor steps out and collapses into the arms of Jackie Tyler and Mickey Smith. A shocked Rose appears at the Tardis doors and tells them that the stranger lying in front of them is, in fact, the Doctor.

As the Doctor sleeps, Prime Minister Harriet Jones gives a press conference about the Guinevere One Space Probe, which had been heading out into space until it was captured by a large rock-like spaceship. Transmissions from the Guinevere space probe resume and reveal a growling alien, called a Sycorax. The Prime Minister and her right-hand man, Alex head to the UNIT base behind the Tower of London. The Sycorax start broadcasting a message to Earth, but nobody can understand it – not even Rose, who can normally use the Tardis' telepathic circuits to communicate in English with alien beings.

The Sycorax then activate a device, and one-third of the world's population falls under their control. The Sycorax ship then enters the Earth's atmosphere and Harriet, Alex and a group of other officials are teleported onboard. Rose and Mickey decide to carry the still unconscious Doctor back into the Tardis. The Sycorax immediately become aware of the ship's presence and also teleport on board their vessel. Unaware of what has happened, Mikey and Rose step out of the Tardis and are confronted by a horde of angry aliens. The Doctor remains unconscious inside the Tardis, as a flask of tea slowly drips into the ship's circuit boards.

As Rose demands the Sycorax leave the Earth alone, she realises she can now understand what they are saying. The Tardis telepathic circuits are working again. She turns around and sees the Doctor, standing there, still wearing his pyjamas and dressing gown. The Doctor distracts the Sycorax leader long enough to free the enslaved humans standing on rooftops and then challenges him to a sword fight. The Doctor eventually wins the fight and orders the Sycorax to leave the Earth, telling them:

...it is protected.

Trivia and facts

Initial ideas for the Christmas special involved Harriet Jones unveiling the rebuilt Big Ben, while a civil servant was making a secret deal with an alien race, possibly the Sycorax, who were named by Russell T. Davies after Caliban's mother in William Shakespeare's 1611 play The Tempest.

Rehearsals for 'The Christmas Invasion' started in Cardiff on 18 July 2005. The cast read-through of the festive special along with the other two episodes of the first filming block took place the following day (19 July). As well as the cast and crew, writers Steven Moffat, Toby Whithouse and Stephen Fry all attended the readthrough to get a flavour of the Tennant's performance. At the time, Fry was working on a script for later in the season, which was subsequently shelved (See 'Fear Her').

While filming on the Brandon Estate in London on 29 July, the Fifth Doctor, Peter Davison visited the set and posed for pictures in front of the Tardis with Tennant. The Doctor makes a passing comment that his dressing gown and pyjamas are 'very Arthur Dent', which is a reference to the character in The

Hitchhiker's Guide to the Galaxy by the late Douglas Adams. The celebrated author was a script editor on Doctor Who during its 17th season, which was originally broadcast in 1979. Adams also wrote three Doctor Who stories during the late 1970s. The Tenth Doctor's pinstripe suit and plimsol trainers were inspired by the TV chef Jamie Oliver, who had appeared alongside Billie Piper as a guest on the ITV chat show Parkinson, wearing a white suit and trainers. When Tennant appeared on the same programme two years later, he said 'the very next morning' he discussed that look with Russell T. Davies and asked if they could do something similar for the Doctor.

'New Earth'

Original UK airdate: 15 April 2006
Cast: David Tennant as The Doctor, Billie Piper as Rose Tyler, Camille Coduri as Jackie Tyler, Noel Clarke as Mickey Smith, Zoe Wanamaker as Cassandra, Sean Gallagher as Chip, Dona Croll as Matron Casp, Michael Fitzgerald as the Duke of Manhattan, Lucy Robinson as Frau Clovis, Adjoa Andoh as Sister Jatt, Anna Hope as Novice Hame, Simon Ludders as the patient and Struan Rodger as the Face of Boe
Written by Russell T. Davies
Directed by James Hawes
Music by Murray Gold
Produced by Phil Collinson
Filming dates: two individual days production took place on 1 and 22 August 2005, while the main filming block ran from 5 September to 26 September. Extra production work took place on 7/8 October and 3 November
Running time: 44 minutes
Original UK viewing figures: 8.6 million

Review

In the days of 'classic' *Doctor Who*, the producers would often bring back a famous monster for the opening story of a series to help boost viewing figures. The team behind the rebooted series used the same trick with Rose, which was the opening episode of the first series by using the Autons from the original era.

Instead, the producers opted to bring back Lady Cassandra from the first series episode 'The End of the World'. This might not have been the most obvious choice in the world, especially as the original story was pretty forgettable, but it did allow Tennant and Piper to flex their comedy muscles in the first half, which is a broad body-swap comedy. Piper, in particular, seems to revel in playing Cassandra, milking lines like 'I'm a chav!' for all their worth. And now free from his previous incarnation's angst over the Time War, the Tenth Doctor is instantly more fun and playful. The kiss between the Doctor and Rose/Cassandra was shameless clickbait for the show's growing legion of new devotees. It also managed to infuriate old school fans, who have still not recovered from a similar snog in the 1996 *Doctor Who TV Movie*. The online fan forums have not been the same since.

But 'New Earth' also proves that this version of the Doctor is not to be underestimated, and as the story lurches into a zombie flick, you see the full force of the Tenth Doctor. The fire and fury bubbles just below the surface, making him the most vengeful Doctor yet. The mish-mash between comedy and horror flick in 'New Earth' works better than it has any right to, but then Doctor Who always could get away with blending genres together. 'New Earth' might lack the dramatic punch of 'The Christmas Invasion' or other stories in series two and feel a bit inconsequential at times, but it remains an entertaining if low key start to the season.

The story

The Doctor and Rose travel 'further than we've ever gone before' to the planet New Earth in the year 5,000,000,023 after the Time Lord receives a message to visit someone in a hospital via his psychic paper. Their arrival is detected by Lady Cassandra, who first appeared in 'The End of the World' and her manservant, Chip. After arriving at the hospital together, the Doctor and Rose become separated after they take different lifts. The Doctor heads up to Ward 26 to discover who sent him the message and Rose goes down to the basement, where she encounters Cassandra and Chip.

Up on Ward 26, the Doctor meets the Sisters of Plenitude, a cat-like race of nurses, who look after the patients. He is also reunited with the Face of Boe, who is dying of old age. One of the nurses, Novice Hame, tells the Doctor legend has it that the Face of Boe will impart a great secret just before his death. Down in the basement, Cassandra activates a machine, which allows her to take over the body of Rose. The possessed Rose then heads up to Ward 26, rejoins the Doctor and promptly kisses him. Growing suspicious of the Sister's medical treatments, the Doctor accesses a computer terminal, which reveals a secret chamber. The chamber contains hundreds of cells, each containing a human being.

The possessed Rose reveals she is Cassandra who sprays the Doctor with a perfume that renders him unconscious. The Doctor wakes up to find he is trapped in one of the cells, as Cassandra threatens to blackmail the Sisters of Plenitude.

When the Sisters refuse to give her money, Cassandra orders Chip to open all the cells in the chamber. Suddenly, hundreds of beings are roaming the hospital and can infect anyone they touch. The Doctor gets all the intravenous solutions to cure every infection, then enters a lift shaft and plummets down the cable with Cassandra. He then pours all the solutions into the lift's decontamination tank. He then jumps into the lift, and as it starts to spray the solution all over him, he urges the hordes to come into the lift and they also get sprayed.

As the carriers become cured, he urges them to get out into the rest of the hospital and pass it on, curing everyone else by touch. The Doctor says goodbye to the Face of Boe, who promises to reveal his secret the next time they meet. Chip re-appears, and Cassandra leaves the body of Rose and possesses her manservant instead. The Doctor and Rose then take Chip/Cassandra back in time to a party, where Cassandra meets her younger self. She tells the younger Cassandra that she looks beautiful and then dies in her arms.

Trivia and facts

The original title for the episode was 'Body Swap'. In the end, 'New Earth' was the final episode in the first block of three to be filmed, following work on 'The Christmas Invasion' and 'School Reunion', both of which took longer to film than originally planned. Explained director James Hawes in the book *Doctor Who: The Inside Story* by Gary Russell:

> New Earth was a nightmare, honestly, where the ambition of the script burst the seams of the budget and the schedule.

According to the 2006 book, the production team were still doing pick-up shots for 'New Earth' while Graeme Harper was directing the Cybermen episodes in November. The outdoor scenes on 'New Earth' were filmed on the Gower Peninsula, near Swansea. Unfortunately for the crew, the scenes were hampered by bad weather during filming and the final scene in the episode, outside the Tardis, had to be abandoned due to a rainstorm.

The party scenes featuring Zoe Wanamaker as Cassandra were filmed in the Ba Orient dim sum restaurant on Mermaid Quay in Cardiff Bay. The hospital foyer scenes were filmed at the Millennium Centre, also in Cardiff Bay, while Tredegar House's cellars were used for Cassandra's lair. And an early version of the script saw the Doctor decide to kill the infected patients off because they were beyond hope. This was later changed after script editor Helen Raynor viewed it as too harsh a decision.

'Tooth and Claw'

Original UK airdate: 22 April 2006
Cast: David Tennant as The Doctor, Billie Piper as Rose Tyler, Pauline Collins as Queen Victoria, Ian Hanmore as Father Angelo, Michelle Duncan as Lady Isobel, Derek Riddell as Sir Robert, Jamie Sives as Captain Reynolds, Ron Donachie as Steward, Tom Smith as the Host and Ruthie Milne as Flora
Written by Russell T. Davies
Directed by Euros Lyn
Music by Murray Gold
Produced by Phil Collinson
Filming dates: production ran from 26 September to 12 October 2005, with additional filming days on 20/26 and 27 October
Running time: 44 minutes
Original UK viewing figures: 9.2 million

Review

With kung fu monks, a castle and a caged werewolf, 'Tooth and Claw' boasts one of the coolest opening scenes in the show's history. Nobody was going to turn over to ITV1 and catch the repeat of *Midsomer Murders* after watching those first three minutes, were they?

Sadly, there's a distinct lack of martial art magic in the rest of the story. Instead, 'Tooth and Claw' is pure gothic horror, which harks back to the days when Phillip Hinchliffe was Doctor Who's showrunner in the mid-1970s and epic tales like 'Pyramids of Mars' and 'The Talons of Weng-Chiang'. The transformation of the werewolf itself was particularly well done and looks good today. If ever there was an episode to finally bury the notion that *Doctor Who* was wobbly sets and actors in ill-fitting rubber suits, then it has to be this one.

The producers were also able to use the natural surroundings of locations of Craig Y Nos Castle to ramp up the tension, with plenty of period details and atmosphere. As the werewolf runs through the castle, picking off soldiers, you cannot help but admire just how good this episode looks. Like all the best Doctor Who episodes, there are a few plot holes in the narrative to bring everything together in the 45-minute running time. The idea that Sir Robert's father and Prince Albert develop a giant telescope and cut a diamond, just to defeat a werewolf in the remote Scottish countryside seems a bit convoluted and does not bear close examination, but this is Doctor Who after all, where such things are commonplace.

Rose's continued attempts to get Queen Victoria to say 'We are not amused' get a bit annoying, and we will gloss over the idea that the royal family are all werewolves for the time being. But 'Tooth and Claw' is still one of the most exciting episodes in the new run thus far. If only they had broadcast this as the opening story, rather than 'New Earth'.

The story

A group of monks, led by Father Angelo, walk over a rugged moor and arrive at an old manor house. They take the house by force and lock Lady Isobel and the servants in the cellar with a hooded figure in a cage. The Doctor tells Rose he is taking her to see Ian Dury and the Blockheads in 1979, but the Tardis materialises in the Scottish countryside in 1879 instead. As they walk out of the Tardis, they are captured by Captain Reynolds and his soldiers, who are escorting a carriage.

The Doctor identifies himself as Doctor James McCrimmon and is invited to speak to the occupant of the carriage, who turns out to be Queen Victoria. The Queen says she is heading to the home of Sir Robert MacLeish and invites the Doctor and Rose to join her. When they arrive at the house, Sir Robert shows Queen Victoria his father's telescope, called Endeavour, as the monks secretly prepare a soup in the kitchen, which they serve to the Queen's guards and it sends them to sleep. Rose discovers a maid, hiding in a cupboard. The maid warns Rose that she is hiding from the monks. But they are both caught by the monks, who drag off them to the cellar.

Upstairs, the Doctor dines with Queen Victoria, Sir Robert and Captain Reynolds. The Queen asks Sir Robert to tell her of a local legend of a wolf, which dates back 300 years. Down in the cellar, Rose quizzes the hooded figure, who reveals he is a host for an alien intelligence and was kidnapped by the monks when he was a young boy.

The figure then tells Rose it plans to migrate to Queen Victoria and create 'the Empire of the Wolf'. In the dining room, Angelo overpowers Captain Reynolds, but Queen Victoria pulls out her own gun and shoots him, as the Doctor and Sir Robert race to find out what is going downstairs. The Doctor, Rose, Queen Victoria and Sir Robert are reunited as the wolf wreaks havoc in the house. They run to the library, where Captain Reynolds stands his ground and holds the wolf at bay long enough for them to barricade themselves in. Inside the library, the Queen reveals she possesses the Koh-i-Noor diamond and the Doctor realises that the house is a trap, specially designed for the wolf by Sir Robert's father.

But then the wolf appears and crashes through the library skylight, forcing them to run to the observatory. The Doctor and Rose position the telescope, so it points towards the moon, while Sir Robert stands guard outside. The wolf kills him and bursts inside but is overpowered by the telescope refracting the moonlight through the telescope and the diamond. The wolf asks the Doctor to make the light brighter, and as he does, the creature dissolves. Afterwards, the Queen dubs her rescuers Sir Doctor of Tardis and Dame Rose of the Powell Estate, and then promptly banishes them. After they leave, the Queen tells Isobel she will establish the Torchwood Institute to fight 'strange happenings'.

Trivia and facts

Another writer was commissioned by showrunner Russell T. Davies to write this episode and was given a brief involving Jack-the-Ripper-style murders, which were being committed around Buckingham Palace. But despite developing a two-page treatment in which Queen Victoria got an alien insect in her eye and the Doctor having to operate, Davies took the commission on himself. He also originally suggested that the song playing in the Tardis at the beginning of the story be the 1979 hit 'Lucky Number' by the American singer Lene Lovich. However, a British artist was easier to clear and so the script was changed to specify that 'Hit Me With Your Rhythm Stick' by Ian Dury and the Blockheads be played instead.

When quizzed by Queen Elizabeth, the Doctor gives his name as Jamie McCrimmon, who travelled with the Second Doctor in the programme between 1966 and 1969. One of his stories 'The Faceless Ones' also featured a young Pauline Collins as Samantha Briggs. Collins was offered the chance to stay on as companion at the end of the story but turned it down. Drama student Josh Green was the stand-in for the CGI werewolf on the set and wore a tight lycra body stocking, which was either white, black or green, depending on the type of shot.

Craig Y Nos Castle in the Brecon Beacons National Park in the Upper Swansea Valley was used to film the front of Torchwood House. The gothic castle has been dubbed the 'Most Haunted Castle in Wales' after having been visited by UkLiving's *Most Haunted* TV programme. The dining room scenes were filmed at Llansannor Court in Llansannor, Vale of Glamorgan, while Tredegar House in Newport provided various kitchen, study and library locations.

'School Reunion'

Original UK airdate: 29 April 2006
Cast: David Tennant as The Doctor, Billie Piper as Rose Tyler, Noel Clarke as Mickey Smith, Anthony Head as Mr Finch, Elisabeth Sladen as Sarah Jane Smith, Rod Arthur as Mr Parsons, Eugene Washington as Mr Wagner, Heather Cameron as Nina, Joe Pickley as Kenny, Benjamin Smith as Luke, Clem Tibber as Milo, Lucinda Dryzek as Melissa, Caroline Berry as Dinner Lady and John Leeson as the voice of K-9
Written by Toby Whithouse
Directed by James Hawes
Music by Murray Gold
Produced by Phil Collinson
Filming dates: production ran from 23 August to 8 September 2005, with an additional filming day on 8 October
Running time: 44 minutes
Original UK viewing figures: 8.3 million

Review

When Russell T. Davies brought *Doctor Who* back to British television screens, he quite sensibly resisted the urge to shovel in as many continuity references to the old show as possible. But 'School Reunion' marks a big change with the return of two iconic characters from 'classic' *Doctor Who*, Sarah Jane Smith and K-9. Cameos can be a risky strategy, particularly when they are just brief walk-ons and played for laughs.

But 'School Reunion' makes a virtue of the show's longevity and answers a question never before asked in its history, what actually happens to companions after they leave the Doctor? Despite being away from the role for many years, Elisabeth Sladen slips effortlessly back into the character. The scene where Sarah Jane and the Doctor meet properly for the first time in the school gymnasium is so beautifully played that even the most die-hard Doctor Who fans would have been sobbing into their keyboards with pure joy. Shame they didn't make her pretend to climb up a grassy hill as they did in the 'The Five Doctors', but you can't have everything.

Rose is clearly jealous at the arrival of the someone from the Doctor's past, and the script milks that point for all its worth, with the subtext of the Doctor and Rose's relationship becoming more blatant with every passing episode.

Somewhere in the middle of all of this are some aliens and their attempts to crack something called the Stasis Paradigm, which is pure guff. At least it gives Anthony Stewart Head free reign to chew the scenery, which he does in the swimming pool scene to devastating effect.

Ultimately, 'School Reunion' is the story of what happens when your girlfriend meets your ex. It's a bit chaotic, but once you've got over the embarrassing bits, it's strangely life-affirming, with a robot dog thrown in for good measure. If there isn't something in your eye as K-9 and Sarah Jane walk off into the sunset at the end, then you are dead inside.

The story

A young girl is sent to see the headmaster of Deffry Vale High School, Mr Finch. She tells him she has no parents and comes from a children's home. The headmaster invites her into his office for lunch. As soon as his office door shuts, she starts to scream. In another part of the school, the Doctor is posing as a new teacher and giving a physics lesson. He is very impressed with the knowledge shown by some of the pupils.

Rose is also working at the school as a dinner lady, following a tip-off from Mickey Smith. Elsewhere, Mr Finch is giving a tour to a journalist, Sarah Jane Smith, who is writing a feature on his achievements. Mr Finch introduces Sarah Jane to the other teachers in the staffroom. The Doctor instantly recognises her and introduces himself as John Smith, but she does not recognise him. Later that night, both Sarah Jane and separately, the Doctor, Mickey and Rose enter the empty building to investigate further. Sarah Jane discovers the Tardis in a storeroom. Stunned, she walks into the gymnasium and encounters the Doctor. However, their reunion is interrupted by the sound of Mickey screaming after he has found some vacuum-packed rats in a cupboard. Sarah Jane takes to the Doctor to her car and shows him another of his old companions, a robot dog called K-9. The gang retire to a café, where the Doctor repairs K-9. The robot dog identifies the cooking oil from the school kitchen as Krillitane oil and the Doctor explains that Krillitanes are a composite race, who cherry-pick various aspects of the creatures they conquer.

The following day, they all return to the school. The Doctor tells Rose and Sarah Jane to examine the computers in the maths room, while he confronts Mr Finch at the swimming pool. Mr Finch tells the other Krillitanes that the time has come to 'initiate the final phase'. All the children are brought inside and set to work on the computers. The Doctor realises the Krillitanes are using the children's imagination to crack the Skasis Paradigm, an ancient code that controls the 'building blocks of the universe'. The aliens are using the cooking oil to boost the children's intelligence.

The Doctor, Rose and Sarah Jane find themselves trapped in the dining room, where they come under attack from the Krillitanes, who have reverted to their bat-like state. Fortunately, K-9 is at hand to defend them. They retreat to the kitchens, where the Doctor realises that Krillitane oil is highly toxic to the

Krillitanes themselves because they have changed their physiology so often. K-9 offers to blow up the vats and oil. The gang leave the robot dog to face Mr Finch and the alien monsters, while they evacuate all the pupils from the school.

When Mr Finch and the Krillitanes enter the kitchen, K-9 fires a laser blast which destroys the alien monsters, himself and most of the school building in the process.

Later, the Doctor shows Sarah Jane inside the Tardis and invites her to travel with him again. She declines, but Mickey asks if he can come along instead. As the Tardis dematerialises, Sarah Jane sees that the Doctor has left her a brand-new K-9 as a parting gift.

Trivia and facts

Showrunner Russell T. Davies originally suggested to writer Toby Whithouse that the story be set on an army camp and a nearby village, where the locals were being turned into scientific geniuses and had started to build a bomb. The story slot was provisionally given the title 'Old Friends'. After a few attempts, Whithouse changed the story to be based in a school, although the idea of aliens doing something to increase the brainpower of human beings for their own ends was retained.

On her second day of filming, Elisabeth Sladen slipped on a polished floor and twisted her ankle, so the third assistant director, Lynsey Muir, complete with a Sarah Jane Smith wig, doubled for her in scenes where her face was not visible.

The majority of the location filming took place at Duffryn High School in Newport, while the Da Vinci's Coffee Shop in Newport's High Street was used for the café scenes.

Director James Hawes got Sladen and Piper to laugh after their scene arguing in the maths room by having Tennant appear with a comedy moustache on his face.

'School Reunion' also saw the return of John Leeson as the voice of K-9, although he was not present for the filming and instead recorded his lines in post-production. Producer Phil Collinson and first assistant director Jon Older read K-9's dialogue live onset. One early draft of the story saw K-9 getting more irritable with age and finished with Rose being rude to the robot dog, which caused him to drive over her foot.

'The Girl in the Fireplace'

Original UK airdate: 6 May 2006
Cast: David Tennant as The Doctor, Billie Piper as Rose Tyler, Noel Clarke as Mickey Smith, Sophia Myles as Reinette, Ben Turner as King Louis, Jessica Atkins as Young Reinette, Angel Coulby as Katherine, Gareth Wyn Griffiths as Manservant, Paul Kasey as Clockwork Man and Ellen Thomas as Clockwork Woman
Written by Steven Moffat
Directed by Euros Lyn
Music by Murray Gold

Produced by Phil Collinson
Filming dates: production ran from 6 October to 27 October 2005
Running time: 44 minutes
Original UK viewing figures: 7.9 million

Review

Full of witty dialogue, spooky monsters and a plot twist that no one (at the time) saw coming, it's easy to look back at 'The Girl in the Fireplace' and see it as a template for Steven Moffat's later tenure as *Doctor Who* showrunner. The story itself is quite bonkers, even by *Doctor Who* standards, with the narrative unfolding simultaneously in 18th century France and a faulty spaceship somewhere in the future.

The theme of monsters under the bed is something that Moffat would return to in the Twelfth Doctor era, particularly in 'Listen' and there's an argument to be made that Madame de Pompadour is the 18th century equivalent of later Moffat characters, like Professor River Song, Clara Oswald and Missy. The idea of two lovers meeting each other at different stages of their lives is another concept that Moffat would return to with River Song and the Eleventh Doctor, played by Matt Smith. Credit must also go to Sophia Myles, who was well cast as the as Madame de Pompadour. Her on-screen, undeniable chemistry is a joy to behold. It's no wonder that Myles and Tennant ended up as an item after acting those scenes. As first dates go, it's hard to beat.

The only flaw, is that while Rose was clearly envious of the Doctor's relationship with Sarah Jane Smith just one episode before ('School Reunion'), she appears to be remarkably unfazed about the arrival of Madame de Pompadour. But maybe that's just nit-picking when the episode is much more focused on the Doctor and his character. Whether it's a template for the later Moffat era or not, 'The Girl in the Fireplace' is also a highly entertaining stand-alone episode, reflecting the growing confidence of everyone involved, both behind the scenes and on the screen.

The story

It is 18th century France and the Palace of Versailles in France is under attack. King Louis warns his mistress Reinette that there are creatures outside and she crouches down to the fireplace in her room and calls to the Doctor for help. Several thousand years later, the Doctor, Rose and Mickey materialise on a deserted alien spaceship. As they walk around the ship, they discover an old fireplace. They crouch down and see a young girl, called Reinette on the other side.

Intrigued, the Doctor finds the switch on the fireplace, which causes it to revolve and he is transported to Reinette's bedroom. But he discovers it is several months since they have just spoken. The Doctor also becomes aware of a loud ticking noise, which is coming from a clockwork robot in an opera mask hiding beneath her bed. The android says Reinette is 'incomplete' and promptly vanishes in front of his eyes. The Doctor returns to Reinette's room, but she is now a young woman. Reinette kisses him passionately and then runs off, leaving the Doctor to realise her true identity, she is none other than the celebrated Madame de Pompadour.

He returns to the ship and finds a horse wandering the corridors. The Doctor catches up with Mickey and Rose and discover that there are time windows on every deck of the ship, all relating to the life of Madame de Pompadour. In one of the windows, they see Reinette about to be attacked by another clockwork robot. The three of them step through the window and freeze the android, which then teleports back to ship. The Doctor sends Mickey and Rose off to investigate, as the Time Lord looks into Reinette's memories. To his surprise, she can also look into his. Back on the ship, Mickey and Rose are captured by more clockwork robots and strapped to operating tables. But before they can operate, the Doctor staggers in, pretending to be drunk. He disables the robots, but they reactivate and teleport away.

The Doctor explains that the ship is 37 years old and when Reinette is 37, the robots will think her brain is 'compatible'.

They find another time window which shows a Versailles ballroom, where Reinette is celebrating her 37th birthday, and the clockwork robots have appeared again. The Doctor rides the horse through the time window and into the ballroom. With the time window smashed, the link between the spaceship and 18th century France is broken, and the androids stop working. The Doctor believes he is now stuck in Versailles with Reinette but then discovers a fireplace which is still connected to the ship.

He returns to the ship and finds his friends. He tells them to get in the Tardis and then uses the fireplace to return to Versailles, in order to bring Reinette back to the future.

But when he arrives, he discovers Reinette is now dead. The Time Lord is given a letter from her, in which she begs her 'lonely angel' to come back to her. The Tardis dematerialises, leaving behind the empty ship, which bears the name SS Madame Du Pompadour.

Trivia and facts

Russell T. Davies gave Steven Moffat the brief of Madame de Pompadour and a clockwork man. Moffatt was initially worried that a historical story would be too boring for younger viewers but then took inspiration from Andrey Niffenegger's 2003 *The Time Traveller's Wife*, where a man travels through time unpredictably. Moffat told the Gothamist website in 2011:

> I said to Russell, 'we should do a *Doctor Who* version of that because that's a perfect fit for us'. Structurally it ended up being different, though.

The original outline for the story had the title 'Madame de Pompadour' and was slated to be the second episode of the 2006 series. Early versions of the script also had the titles 'Every Tick of My Heart' and 'Reinette and the Lonely Angel', before Moffat eventually settled on 'The Girl in the Fireplace'.

The scene where the Doctor crashes through the mirror and into the Versailles ballroom presented several challenges for the film crew. Some parts of the scene were filmed in Ragley Hall in Alcester, Warwickshire, which is home to the Marquess and Marchioness of Hereford. Because using a real horse in Ragley Hall was deemed impractical, Tennant instead sat atop a small piece of scaffolding rig, which was then wheeled around by the crew.

This footage was then mixed with material filmed at David Broom's Event Centre in Chepstow, where a large greenscreen was erected for footage of both Tennant and stunt double Peter Miles riding a show-jumping horse called Arthur. A different horse was used for the scenes onboard the spaceship and was called Bolero, who looked similar to Arthur but was more suited for working on a confined set. And Dyffryn Gardens in the Vale of Glamorgan doubled for the external shots of the Palace of Versailles.

'Rise of the Cybermen/The Age of Steel'

Original UK airdate: 13/20 May 2006
Cast: David Tennant as The Doctor, Billie Piper as Rose Tyler, Camille Coduri as Jackie Tyler, Noel Clarke as Mickey Smith, Shaun Dingwall as Pete Tyler, Roger Lloyd Pack as John Lumic, Andrew Hayden-Smith as Jake Simmonds, Don Warrington as the President, Mona Hammond as Rita-Anne, Helen Griffin as Mrs Moore, Colin Spaull as Mr Crane, Paul Anthony Barber as Dr Kendrick, Adam Shaw as Morris, Andrew Ufondo as Soldier, Duncan Duff as Newsreader, Paul Kasey as Cyber Leader and Nicholas Briggs as the voice of the Cybermen
Written by Tom MacRae
Directed by Graeme Harper
Music by Murray Gold
Produced by Phil Collinson
Filming dates: production ran from 1 November to 16 December, 2005, before a break for Christmas. It then resumed in the New Year, with production from 7 January to 18 January 2006, with additional filming days on 18/22 February and 9 March
Running time: 46/45 minutes
Original UK viewing figures: 9.2/7.6 million

Review

Having successfully rebooted the Daleks in the first series of *Doctor Who*, it was only a matter of time before Russell T. Davies turned his attention to another of programme's most enduring enemies, the Cybermen. Rather wisely, the showrunner took the opportunity to ditch some of the more confusing aspects of the Cybermen's mythology. Out went the Cybermen's homeworld of Mondas, not to mention the other homeworld of Telos. Yes, you read that right. It's a sore point amongst some fans. Best not to mention the Cryons from 'Attack of the Cybermen', either.

Instead, an alternative reality and a megalomaniac, played with some relish by the late Roger Lloyd-Pack was devised. The design of the Cybermen themselves also had an upgrade, with the monsters now looking like they were actually made of steel, as opposed toa bunch of blokes in silver ski boots and flight suits. They also became a lot less melodramatic than their 1980s counterparts, with a colder, mechanical voice supplied by Nicholas 'Voice of the Daleks' Briggs.

The two-parter also gives Noel Clarke a chance to shine in the twin roles of Mickey and Ricky Smith. Up until this point, Mickey Smith has been largely kept on the sidelines, but this story sees the character step out and become his own man.

Putting Rose in a maid's outfit does feel a bit 'something for the dads', although putting the Doctor in a dinner jacket presumably went down well in other quarters too. Away from the monsters themselves, the story benefits from the return of director Graeme Harper, who also produced one of the finest Doctor Who stories in the 1980s, 'The Caves of Androzani'. Harper has a natural flair for action sequences, and the entrance of the Cybermen at the end of the first episodes looks straight out of a Hollywood movie. Harper also made the Cybermen scary again, and for that, we should all be thankful.

The story

The Doctor, Rose and Mickey arrive on a parallel world, which is similar to their own, but with some big differences, like Zeppelins flying across the skies of London. In this parallel world, an industrialist John Lumic is working on a prototype for a cybernetic life form and Rose's father Pete Tyler is still alive. He is now a successful entrepreneur and living with his wife, Jackie, in a large country house. Everyone also wears ear pods, which give them a daily download of news, sport and weather from Lumic's company Cybus Industries. The pods also give Lumic full access to people's memories. Lumic unveils his prototype to the President of Great Britain, who refuses to give it his permission.

Mickey realises his grandmother is still alive in the parallel world, so sets off to find her, but he is kidnapped by Jake and another activist, Moore. They take Mickey back to their secret base, where he meets the leader of their gang – Mickey's parallel counterpart, Ricky. The Doctor and Rose bluff their way into Jackie Tyler's 40th birthday party. Suddenly, floodlights come on and illuminate an army of Cybermen marching towards the house. The Cybermen smash through the French windows and terrify the party-goers, including the President of Great Britain who is "deleted" by the metal monsters.

The Doctor, Rose and Pete flee from the chaos and are met by Mickey, Ricky and Jake outside. They are then surrounded by Cybermen who start chanting 'Delete! Delete! Delete!' The Doctor uses a Tardis power cell to stun the Cybermen and the gang escape. As they flee the scene, Pete reveals that he has been trying to help Ricky's rebel group. Lumic sends a signal that puts everybody wearing ear pods in London into a hypnotic trance. The Cybermen start rounding the hypnotised people up and take them to Battersea Power Station, which has become a factory for converting them into more Cybermen.

The gang split up. Ricky is electrocuted by the Cybermen. The Doctor and Moore get into the power station through the cooling tunnels, while Rose and Pete go through the front door pretending to be hypnotised. Jake and Mickey head to the Zeppelin on top of the station. The Cybermen convert John Lumic and turn him into their Cyber Controller. They also capture Pete, Rose and the Doctor, and kill Moore. They are all taken to the control room, where they meet the Controller.

Onboard the Zeppelin, Mickey picks up a signal from the control room. Listening in to the conversation, he realises the Doctor is talking to him and telling him where to find the emotional inhibitor cancellation code, which could disable all the Cybermen. Mickey finds the code and sends it to Rose's phone, which the Doctor is able to plug into the control systems. As the code signal destroys all the Cybermen, the Doctor, Pete and Rose escape on the Zeppelin, which is being piloted by Jake and Mickey.

With the Cybermen defeated, Mickey tells Rose he will stay in this parallel world with his gran. The Doctor and Rose depart in the Tardis and return to her universe, as Mickey and Jake head off on another adventure.

Trivia and facts

The two-part story was partly inspired by a *Big Finish* audio adventure, 'Spare Parts' by Marc Platt. Originally released in 2002 and featuring the Fifth Doctor, Peter Davison, it was set on the Cybermen's homeworld of Mondas and shows how its inhabitants submitted themselves to the conversion process as a means of survival.

Writer Tom MacRae used 'Spare Parts' as the starting point, but as work on the story progressed it became more about downloads and upgrades.

In the original story idea, Pete Tyler was a government collaborator, and Mickey was the leader of the rebels. MacRae also wanted to make the Cybermen more terrifying by emphasising the fact that they do not kill their victims, and instead convert them. The notion that Cybermen want to 'upgrade' human beings came later in the scriptwriting process after MacRae and Davies broke the story down.

The dummy company run by the character of John Lumic is called International Electromatics, which is also the same name as the firm run by Tobias Vaughan in the 1968 Cybermen adventure 'The Invasion'.

The filming of 'Rise of the Cybermen/The Age of Steel' also saw the return of director Graeme Harper to Doctor Who. Harper had previously directed Peter Davison's swansong 'The Caves of Androzani' in 1984, which was rated by readers of Doctor Who Magazine in 2014 as the fourth greatest story of all time. He also directed 'Revelation of the Daleks' in 1985, starring the Sixth Doctor, Colin Baker, and was a production assistant on 'Warrior's Gate' in 1980, which featured the Fourth Doctor, Tom Baker. Harper has also known actor Colin Spaull, who played Mr Crane since they were both ten years old and also cast him in 'Revelation of the Daleks'.

A private house at St Nicholas, near Cardiff, was used as the location for the Tyler's country mansion, Uskmouth Power Station in Newport doubled for Battersea Power Station in London and a Stella Artois brewery at Wilcrick was used for the upgrade chamber sequences.

The 'blue tooth' ear pods did prove to be a challenge for some of the cast members. In the DVD episode commentary, Noel Clarke admitted: '...people had a lot of problems and they kept falling out'. Like many of the Doctor Who stories set in London, the production crew always used fake street signs to hide the fact they were actually filming in Wales. However, if you watch the final scene where Mickey and Jake drive off in the van, you will see they drive past a sign that clearly says 'Welcome to Newport'.

'The Idiot's Lantern'
Original UK airdate: 27 May 2006
Cast: David Tennant as The Doctor, Billie Piper as Rose Tyler, Maureen Lipman as The Wire, Ron Cook as Magpie, Jamie Foreman as Eddie Connolly, Debra Gillett as Rita Connolly, Rory Jennings as Tommy Connolly, Margaret John as Grandma Connolly, Sam Cox as Detective Inspector Bishop, Ieuan Rhys as Crabtree, Jean Challis as Aunty Betty, Christopher Driscoll as Security Guard and Marie Lewis as Mrs Gallagher
Written by Mark Gatiss
Directed by Euros Lyn
Music by Murray Gold
Produced by Phil Collinson
Filming dates: there was an individual filming day on 23 January 2006, while the main production ran from 7 February to 23 February 2006
Running time: 45 minutes
Original UK viewing figures: 6.7 million

Review
The frustrating thing about The Idiot's Lantern is that while there's an awful lot going for it, it never quite achieves classic status. Writer Mark Gatiss gets to indulge his love of 1950s horror stereotypes, such as men in black and faceless human beings and shoehorn in a bit of domestic drama with a bullying father at the same time. It's all a bit *Quatermass and the Pit* meets *Coronation Street*.

Maureen Lipman also gets to make the most of what little she has to do or say at the villainous Wire and the production team recreate the coronation period, especially the coronation street parties, perfectly.

The problem lies with resolving the various plot holes within the 45-minute running time. Tommy Connolly's issues with his overbearing father, which dominate the first quarter of the story, seem to be wrapped up with some haste, although that's nothing compared to the relative ease with which the Doctor defeats the Wire.

She puts herself in a box, so Magpie has to climb up the Alexandra Palace transmitter, so the Doctor then cobbles his own a box of tricks together and follows Magpie in hot pursuit. The Doctor plugs his own box in and et voila! The Wire is trapped in a Betamax cassette. He should have saved himself the bother and plugged it in at the bottom of the tower. Why does nobody ever think to do that?

The scenes at the top of the transmitter do not look very convincing, either. In one of the series' few production fails, both the Doctor and Magpie appear to be holding on to a bit of metalwork on Cardiff heliport, which is where the scene was actually filmed, rather than dangling hundreds of metres up in the air. 'The Idiot's Lantern' feels more like a placeholder than a tentpole episode, providing a brief respite from some of series two's bigger adventures.

The story

It's London 1953 and a struggling electrical shop owner, Magpie, is visited by a well-spoken television announcer who sends lightning bolts out from the television screen and grabs his face. Shortly afterwards, the Doctor and Rose materialise in North London. The Time Lord promised her a trip to see Elvis perform on the Ed Sullivan show, which was in 1957, but as usual, the Tardis had other ideas.

As they walk down the street, they meet the Connolly family, but then they see an old woman bundled into a police car, which speeds off down the road. Young Tommy Connolly tells the Doctor and Rose 'people are turning into monsters'. The Doctor and Rose give chase, but the police car disappears. They return back to the Connolly's house. Wife Rita tries to tell them about her mother, but husband Eddie stops her, but then they hear the sound of banging and race upstairs.

Tommy shows the Doctor and Rose what has happened to his gran – her face has vanished. But before they can properly examine her, policemen burst in and take the grandmother away in a car.

The Doctor follows in hot pursuit and breaks into a yard, where he discovers a cage full of faceless people. Rose heads to Magpie Electricals to quiz the shop owner, but then the announcer appears on one of its television sets. Lightning starts to zap out of the set and grabs Rose's face. The Doctor is caught by Detective Inspector Bishop, who explains they started finding faceless people a month ago. Then another faceless person is brought in, and this time it's Rose. The following morning, the Doctor appears on the Connolly's doorstep and tells Tommy he needs his help. His father intervenes and loses his temper, but Rita stands up to him and tells Tommy to go with the Doctor. The Doctor, Tommy and Bishop break into Magpie's shop, where they find the missing faces are trapped inside the screens. The announcer, known as the Wire, appears in one of the screens and says she intends to use the coronation to regain her physical body.

The Wire attempts to take the faces of the Doctor, Tommy and Bishop but is forced to stop. She transfers her being into a small black box, which Magpie takes to the transmitter at Alexandra Palace. The alien creature intends to feed on everyone watching the Coronation. The Doctor sets off in hot pursuit and climbs up the transmitter and traps the Wire in a hastily-built contraption. All the faceless people have their faces restored including Rose, and London is able to celebrate the Coronation.

Trivia and facts

Showrunner Russell T. Davies originally pitched Mark Gatiss an idea called 'Mr Sandman', which was about an alien intelligence searching for an identity hidden in a 1950s rock and roll song. Gatiss tried to include several references to the popular *Quatermass* science-fiction serials of the 1950s in his script. *The Quatermass Experiment* was broadcast live from Alexandra Palace in 1953, near where 'The Idiot's Lantern' is set. However, the only reference which made it into the finished programme was the clenching hands of the faceless people, which mirrored the possessed Carroon in *The Quartermass Experiment*.

Tennant and Gatiss appeared together in a 2005 revival of *The Quatermass Experiment*, which also starred Jason Flemyng, who is the son of Gordon Flemyng, who directed the Peter Cushing *Doctor Who* movies in the 1960s. In the story, the Connolly family live on Florizel Street, which was the working title for *Coronation Street* back in 1960. The scenes featuring Maureen Lipman were filmed at Alexandra Palace itself, as the actress lived nearby in Muswell Hill, while the Florizel Street scenes were shot on Florentia Street in Cathays.

A blue 1951 Bedford S-Type removal van was parked across one of the junctions on Florentia Street to hide some of the modern cars, which were parked in the area.

Margaret John, who played Grandma Connolly also appeared in 1968's Second Doctor adventure 'Fury from the Deep' as Megan Jones. And the Wire, as played by Maureen Lipman, is closely modelled on the British TV presenter Sylvia Peters, one of the BBC's primary continuity announcers from 1947 to 1958.

'The Impossible Planet/The Satan Pit'

Original UK airdate: 3/10 June 2006
Cast: David Tennant as The Doctor, Billie Piper as Rose Tyler, Danny Webb as Mr Jefferson, Shaun Parkes as Zachary Cross Flane, Claire Rushbrook as Ida Scott, Will Thorp as Toby Zed, Ronny Jhutti as Danny Bartok, MyAnna Buring as Scooti Manista, Paul Kasey as The Ood, Gabriel Woolf as the voice of The Beast and Silas Carson as the voice of the Ood
Written by Matt Jones
Directed by James Strong

Music by Murray Gold
Produced by Phil Collinson
Filming dates: production ran from 28 February to 31 March 2006, with pick-up
filming days 1/4/11 April
Running time: 45/47 minutes
Original UK viewing figures: 6.3/6 million

Review

Stories involving a base manned by a small, plucky crew being picked off by
a larger alien menace were a staple of *Doctor Who* during its classic run from
1963 to 1989.
'The Impossible Planet/The Satan Pit' marks the return of the 'base under
siege' formula, except this time the menace is none other than the Devil
himself. Or is it?

The great thing about the 'base under siege' concept is that it lends
itself particularly well to *Doctor Who*, and this time around no cliché gets
left behind, with a battle-hardened security officer, crew members getting
possessed and a rocket ship for the survivors to escape in.

Writer Matt Jones also gets to have some fun with the script, in particular by
answering the age-old question – why don't the Doctor and the companion just
leg it at the first sight of trouble? Having the Tardis fall down a pit and leaving
the Doctor and Rose stranded helps to add to the tension, which slowly builds
up over the course of its first half to one of the series' finest cliffhangers. And
almost uniquely, the second half does not suffer from the wheels falling off.
The tension continues to build and the story unfolds in an orderly and not-
rushed manner. Even the presence of several big philosophical speeches by the
Tenth Doctor cannot derail 'The Satan Pit' as it marches to its conclusion.

The slave-like Oods also proved to be a big hit as soon as the episodes were
broadcast, making them one of the first 'classic' monsters of the rebooted
series. Bearing in mind that the CGI at the time was never designed for Blu-
Ray or High Definition viewing, the Beast still looks rather impressive. Gabriel
Woolf also gets to scare a new generation of viewers as the voice of the Beast.
It's a shame he does not get anything quite as melodramatic to say as when
he was Sutekh in 1975's 'Pyramids of Mars', but we will gloss over that. 'The
Impossible Planet/The Satan Pit' might not be original, but like all the best
rollercoaster rides, it leaves you wanting more.

The story

The Tardis materialises on Sanctuary Base Six, where Rose sees graffiti that
bears the message 'Welcome to Hell'. The space station is full of servant-like
creatures, called the Ood and a small human crew. The base's head of security,
Jefferson, takes the Doctor and Rose to the main control room, where they
meet the rest of crew. Captain Zachary Cross Flane explains the base is on a
planet orbiting a black hole and there is a power source 10 miles below them,

which they are drilling down to find.

There is an earthquake and part of the base, including the Tardis, falls through a crevasse. Archaeologist Toby Zed is examining a piece of pottery when he starts to hear a sinister voice. The voice tells him not to turn around, and then he sees ancient writing on his hands and face. The drilling stops and the Doctor volunteers to go down to investigate with another crew member, Ida. At the bottom of the lift, they find a vast cavern. Meanwhile, something strange is happening with the Ood. The strength of their telepathic field is increasing and has now reached 100. The Doctor and Ida discover a trapdoor. Via the radio, Toby tells them he knows what it is and then the trapdoor starts to open. Up in the base, the Ood go mad, but the trapdoor itself reveals a bottomless pit.

A voice starts to speak through the Ood. The Doctor asks the voice to identify itself and it replies that it is the Devil, chained in the pit before the universe was created.

The Ood start trying to break into the base control room. Danny decides to jam the Ood's telepathic field, but in order to do this, they will have to get to the part of the base where the Ood normally live. After jamming the field, the crew head to the base's rocket, which then takes off. The Doctor descends to the bottom of the pit, where he discovers two urns and an enormous creature, which resembles a devil. He realises that if he destroys the urns, he will also destroy the gravity funnel, so he smashes them. As the planet is drawn into a black hole, the Doctor finds the Tardis. He uses it to rescue Ida and tow the rocket to safety. After reuniting all the crewmates, the Doctor and Rose are reunited and head off in the Tardis.

Facts and trivia

Russell T. Davies originally wanted a two-part story, which would have plunged the Doctor and Rose into a hostile environment on a desolate planet. The showrunner also wanted a story that would challenge the Doctor's scientific beliefs. Writer Matt Jones original cliff-hanger to the first episode was to have Rose announcing 'I am the Beast incarnate'.The second episode would then have started on the Powell Estate, with Jackie and Mickey behaving strangely, but this would then all appear to be a dream in Rose's mind.

The story went through many drafts and at one point included the Toclafane, who had originally been developed as a possible replacement for the Daleks in series one and would eventually appear in series three ('Last of the Time Lords').

It was the last story of series two to be filmed. Tennant and Piper's last scenes were filmed on 31 March 2006 on the set of the Tardis. The series two wrap party was held later that night at the Number 10 club in Cardiff. It was also the last time the Tardis set was filmed in the Q2 Unit on Imperial Way near Newport since production on Doctor Who started in 2004.

It was then transported to the series' new home at the purpose-built studios at Upper Boat, near Cardiff for work on the following series. 'The Impossible Planet/The Satan Pit' also saw the return of actor Gabriel Woolf to Doctor Who. Woolf provided the voice for Sutekh in the 1975 story 'Pyramids of Mars', opposite Tom Baker and was the voice of The Beast in this story. The Daily Star had claimed at the time that Billie Piper's former husband Chris Evans was being lined up for his role, which just goes to show you should not believe everything you read in the tabloids.

While filming night shoots in Wenvoe Quarry, the crew were amused to see that the last three letters of the quarry manager's Land Rover number plate were OOD. During the filming, the crew also returned to Clearwell Caves near Coleford, Gloucestershire, which had been first used in 'The Christmas Invasion'.

'Love & Monsters'

Original UK airdate: 17 June 2006
Cast: David Tennant as The Doctor, Billie Piper as Rose Tyler, Camille Coduri as Jackie Tyler, Peter Kay as Victor Kennedy/Abzorbaloff, Marc Warren as Elton Pope, Shirley Henderson as Ursula Blake, Simon Greenhall as Mr Skinner, Moya Brady as Bridget, Kathryn Drysdale as Bliss, Paul Kasey as The Hoix and Bella Emberg as Mrs Croot
Written by Russell T. Davies
Directed by Dan Zeff
Music by Murray Gold
Produced by Phil Collinson
Filming dates: production ran from 19 March to 31 March 2006
Running time: 45 minutes
Original UK viewing figures: 6.6 million

Review

Depending on your viewpoint, *'Love & Monsters'* is either a harmless bit of fun or Russell T. Davies having a sly dig at some of the more unsavoury aspects of *Doctor Who* fandom. This is because a lot of people took offence when *'Love & Monsters'* was first broadcast in 2006. Admittedly, most of that umbrage came from the sort of person who spends hours online, moaning that the current *Doctor Who* showrunner has ruined their childhood and they are never watching the show again. Except that they will, obviously.

To explain this hypothesis further, Elton Pope is a regular fan, who just wants to find out more about this favourite programme, have some fun and meet new friends. Victor Kennedy is the 'superfan' who ruins it for everyone, particularly when it comes to posting on online forums. Got that? Good. Then we can carry on.

The episode was originally devised as one which would not require too much of either David Tennant and Billie Piper, so two stories could be filmed at the same time. The production team used the same trick in the following series, with 'Blink' being another 'doctor lite' episode. But 'Love & Monsters' is not in the same league as 'Blink'. 'Love & Monsters' is very silly at times, which may also have enraged some people. Some of the black humour might go over the casual viewer's head. There are several moments which are played purely for laughs, and that's before Peter Kay turns up as Victor Kennedy and the Abzorbaloff. But Marc Warren and Shirley Henderson are very sweet as the star-crossed lovers, Elton Pope and Ursula Blake, and Camille Coduri gets to flesh out the character of Jackie Tyler.

It might not be hard-stopping drama or anything that vaguely resembles science fiction, but 'Love & Monsters' has a certain charm. It also contains several Electric Light Orchestra songs, but don't let that put you off.

The story

Elton Pope scrambles through an industrial wasteland and discovers the Tardis, standing in the middle of nowhere. As he approaches it, he hears Rose scream for the Doctor and runs into an abandoned warehouse. There he finds a terrifying alien, called the Hoix. Later at home, he records a video diary in which he recalls that he first met the Doctor when he was a little boy, after finding him in his living room in the middle of the night. Elton and a woman called Ursula Blake meet a group of like-minded individuals, who are interested in the Doctor, including Mr Skinner, Bridget and a girl called Bliss. They call themselves LINDA and soon become close friends, evening forming a band.

But one day, a man called Victor Kennedy walks into one of LINDA's meetings and takes charge of the group. He starts to give them tasks to catch the Doctor.

When Elton reports he failed to catch the Doctor after one sighting, Victor is furious and then suggests they start to search for the Time Lord's companion. Elton meets an old lady, who identifies Rose from a photograph and gives him Jackie Tyler's address.

Elton strikes up a rapport with Jackie, but when she finds a photo of Rose in Elton's coat pocket, she accuses him of using her to get to the Doctor. Several members of the group start to disappear. One night, Ursula realises she has left her phone behind after a meeting. Elton and her return to find Victor has transformed into a hideous alien called the Abzorbaloff. He has also absorbed Mr Skinner, Bridget and Bliss. He then grabs Ursula and absorbs her too. Elton runs off and the Abzorbaloff gives chase. The Tardis then materialises and the Doctor and Rose emerge.

The Time Lord says the absorbed members of LINDA could use their minds to suppress the alien's willpower. As they do, he drops his cane. Ursula prompts Elton to break the cane, which causes the Abzorbaloff to melt into the ground. The Doctor then explains to Elton that he was in his living room all those years ago, to stop a living shadow, but he was too late, and the shadow killed Elton's mother.

The Doctor then brings back Ursula in the form of a paving stone. Ursula and

Elton live happily ever after.

Facts and trivia

Russell T. Davies's original outline for the story was entitled 'I Love The Doctor', which would feature an obsessed stalker who kept appearing in the Time Lord's life.

The inspiration for this storyline came from a 1999 episode of *Buffy the Vampire Slayer*, entitled 'The Zeppo', in which the character of Xander takes centre stage, while an adventure featuring the rest of the cast takes place largely off-camera.

Stand-up comic and actor Peter Kay wrote Davies a six-page letter after the first series of Doctor Who was broadcast in 2005, saying how much he had enjoyed it. Davies then wrote back to Kay, asking if he would be interested in appearing in the following series.

It was also the last episode of series two to be written, which allowed Davies to incorporate the winning design of a Blue Peter competition for viewers to design the monster in the story. The competition was launched on 19 July 2005, and the closing date for entries was 6 August. It received 43,920 entries and the results were announced on 17 August, when the Tenth Doctor himself, David Tennant announced the winner, from a shortlist of three entries, live on air. The winning entry was the Abzorbaloff, which was created by nine-year-old William Grantham.

Grantham was accompanied by Blue Peter presenter Konnie Huq to watch some of the episode being made on Monday, 27 March 2006 and met Peter Kay, who played Victor Kennedy and the evil Abzorbaloff.

In the story, the group of fans led by Elton called themselves LINDA, which was an acronym first used by Davies when he worked on the BBC1 children's programme Why Don't You? in the 1980s. Back then, it stood for the Liverpool Investigation 'N' Detective Agency, whereas in 'Love & Monsters' it was the London Investigation 'N' Detective Agency.

'Fear Her'

Original UK airdate: 24 June 2006
Cast: David Tennant as The Doctor, Billie Piper as Rose Tyler, Nina Sosanya as Trish, Abisola Agbaje as Chloe, Edna Dore as Maeve, Tim Faraday as Tom's Dad, Abdul Salis as Kel, Ricard Nichols as the Driver, Erica Eirian as the Neighbour, Stephen Marzella as the Police Officer and Huw Edwards as the Commentator
Written by Matthew Graham
Directed by Euros Lyn
Music by Murray Gold
Produced by Phil Collinson
Filming dates: production ran from 24 January to 23 February 2006
Running time: 43 minutes
Original UK viewing figures: 7.1 million

Review

Every season of *Doctor Who* has an episode that either fails to hit the mark and is swiftly forgotten about. In the case of the Tenth Doctor's first series, it is 'Fear Her'. But don't just take my word for it. When *Doctor Who Magazine* asked readers in 2014 to rate every story from the show's first 50 years, 'Fear Her' scored the lowest result of any episode from the modern era, and the second-lowest of all time, coming an impressive 240th out of 241.

Even after all these years, 'Fear Her' still feels like the episode where the production team ran out of cash and had to cobble something together at the last minute, which is a shame as hopes were high at the time that writer Matthew Graham would deliver a classic tale for the revived series.

Graham was well known at the time as the co-creator Life On Mars, which saw a modern-day police officer, Sam Tyler, played by John (The Master) Simm go back in time to 1973, where he meets a charismatic copper called Gene Hunt. Graham was a huge fan of Doctor Who and in the early 2000s is reported to have pitched bringing the show back to the BBC as a gothic-style fantasy, before Russell T. Davies was eventually commissioned as showrunner for the revived series.

'What we had set out to do right from the start with 'Fear Her' was tell a story that was aimed very much at children,' Graham told the website Den of Geek in 2011. 'For children, not really for adults, not really for the older Doctor Who fans.'

This may go some way to explain its notoriety, particularly amongst Doctor Who fans, who swiftly forgot about it, particularly with the epic series finale 'Army of Ghosts/Doomsday' just around the corner. Even so, some of the subject matter feels a little dark for something aimed at younger children. After all these years, it still feels like a rare misstep in what is otherwise an incredibly strong series.

The story

The Tardis brings the Doctor and rose to Dame Kelly Holmes Close, on the outskirts of London, as the nation prepares for the 2012 Olympics. But instead of celebrations, they find several posters for missing children and a community in fear. A streetworker tells Rose how cars keep breaking down in the close, while an old lady called Maeve says that young boys have vanished into air and begs the Doctor and Rose to help them.

Inside one of the houses, a young girl called Chloe sits in a bedroom full of drawings and then draws a cat she has seen in the garden. Rose spots the same cat and follows it, but the creature suddenly vanishes. Upstairs, Chloe grows frustrating and starts drawing a large scribble. As Rose walks around the estate, she is suddenly attacked by a big ball scribble, which the Doctor is able to defeat with his sonic screwdriver.

The Doctor and Rose visit the home of Chloe and speak to her mother, Trish, who asks if they can help her. She says Chloe stays in her room all the time.

Chloe's father died a year ago. Rose goes upstairs to investigate and finds Chloe's room is full of drawings and finds a large sketch of Chloe's father at the back of her cupboard, that growls 'I'm coming to hurt you'. The Doctor says Chloe is harnessing ionic energy to turn the local children into drawings and that 'if living things can become drawings, then maybe drawings can become living things'.

The Doctor attempts to speak to the entity that has possessed Chloe, called Isolus. The creature crashed to Earth on a pod and was drawn to Chloe because she was also lonely. The Doctor and Rose head back to the Tardis to build a gadget, which will locate the crashed pod. But Chloe follows them and starts drawing the Tardis. After the Doctor and Rose emerge from the ship, it vanishes along with the Doctor and the device itself is smashed.

Rose races back to Chloe's bedroom and begs the little girl to bring the Doctor back. She heads outside to find Kel, who tells her he filled in a pothole six days ago. She realises the heat of the tarmac must have attracted the Isolus and that the pod is buried underneath the road. She starts digging up the road and finds the Isolus spaceship.

As the Olympics opening ceremony starts, Chloe starts to draw the stadium and all the spectators and athletes vanish. Rose breaks down the bedroom door and tells the Isolus she has found its pod. Chloe says it needs heat. Rose rushes back into the street, where the Olympic torchbearer is running by and throws the pod into the Olympic flame. The Isolus leaves Chloe and flies back to the pod. The missing children all re-appear, along with the crowd in the Olympic stadium. The torchbearer collapses, but the Doctor picks up the flame and lights the Olympic flame himself.

Trivia and facts

The 11th episode of this series was originally due to have been written by actor, writer and all-round genius Stephen Fry. According to Doctor Who: The Complete History, the episode was provisionally assigned as 'The 1920s'. Fry completed a script, but it was then deemed to be too expensive, and a decision was made to hold it for the following year. However, Fry was then too busy filming the ITV drama Kingdom and unable to complete the necessary rewrites, so his story was abandoned.

Fry was not the only celebrity author rumoured to have been involved in this era. For years, there were rumours that Harry Potter author J.K. Rowling had written a script for the Tenth Doctor, which never made it to screen. Fans may simply have got their wires crossed with another idea Russell T. Davies had for pairing the Tenth Doctor with the actual writer (see 'The Next Doctor').

Speaking at the BFI in London in April 2017, Russell T. Davies's successor, Stephen Moffat confirmed there was indeed a story, which would have brought the worlds of Doctor Who and wizards together. Moffat said:

There was something that was kicked back and forward, but it never got anywhere, It might exist on some hard drive somewhere, but you would have to ask Russell.

In the end, the production team turned to a story by Matthew Graham, which had been commissioned as a self-contained story for either the 2006 or 2007 series. Page Drive, which is off Pallet Way in Tremorfa in Cardiff, became Dame Kelly Holmes Close for the duration of filming, while St. Albans Rugby Club in Tremorfa Park doubled as the Olympic Stadium for the scenes where the Doctor lights the Olympic flame.

'Army of Ghosts/Doomsday'

Original UK airdate: 1/8 July 2006
Cast: David Tennant as The Doctor, Billie Piper as Rose Tyler, Camille Coduri as Jackie Tyler, Noel Clarke as Mickey Smith, Tracy-Ann Oberman as Yvonne Hartman, Raji James as Dr. Rajesh Singh, Freema Agyeman as Adeola, Hadley Fraser as Gareth, Oliver Mellor as Matt, Barbara Windsor as Peggy Mitchell, Derek Acorah as Himself, Alistair Appleton as Himself, Trisha Goddard as Herself, Paul Kasey as the Cyber Leader, Nicholas Briggs as the voices of the Daleks and the Cybermen, Shaun Dingwall as Pete Tyler, Andrew Hayden-Smith as Jake Simmonds, and introducing Catherine Tate as the Bride.
Written by Russell T. Davies
Directed by Graeme Harper
Music by Murray Gold
Produced by Phil Collinson
Filming dates: production ran from 2 November to 15 December 2005 and then paused for a Christmas break. It then resumed on 3 January 2006 and ran until 20 January, with additional filming days on 27 January, 9 March, 31 March and 11 April 2006
Running time: 43/46minutes
Original UK viewing figures: 8.1/8.2million

Review

In the run-up to the broadcast of the finale, it was well-known by the general public that Billie Piper would be leaving the show at the end of series two. Showrunner Russell T. Davies certainly pulled out all the stops for the two-part story, not only giving Rose Tyler one of the most memorable exists in *Doctor Who's* history, but also pulling off one or two surprises in the process.

While everyone knew the Cybermen would be returning in the finale, the arrival of the Daleks took many viewers by surprise, having been kept closely under wraps by the production team. And yes, this is the first time both adversaries have faced each other in Doctor Who, which meant an end to all those online debates and playground fights about which was tougher with some of the most impressive scenes in the show to date. We always knew the Daleks would win, right?

Despite the epic nature of the finale, Davies was also able to tie up all the loose ends from the series, including the recurring motif of the Torchwood Institute, along with the return of Mickey Smith and Pete Tyler. But the finale will always be remembered for those scenes on Bad Wolf Bay as the Tenth Doctor and Rose Tyler are separated forever. More than a decade on, it still brings a tear to the eye as Tennant and Piper give their goodbyes all they are worth.

But as the episode draws to a poignant close, the production team had one final secret in the shape of Catherine Tate on board the Tardis. Given the sheer amount of tabloid scrutiny that continues to plague the show to this very day, to pull two surprises out of the hat takes some doing. 'Army of Ghosts/Doomsday' remains one of the finest finales in the history of Doctor Who, with the Tenth Doctor pushed to the very limit in a story that has huge consequences for the Time Lord and the ongoing continuity.

The story

The Doctor and Rose return to modern-day Earth. An excited Jackie Tyler announces that they have turned just up in time to see Rose's Grandad, who died ten years ago. A few moments later, a ghostly figure appears in Jackie's kitchen. The Doctor races outside and there are ghosts everywhere, but they soon disappear.

In a tower in central London, Yvonne Hartman congratulates the staff of the Torchwood Institute on another successful ghost shift.

Later on, two of Yvonne's team, Adeola and Gareth sneak off for a secret assignation in another part of the building. Gareth vanishes behind some sheeting, and when Adeola looks for him, she encounters a Cyberman. Meanwhile, the Doctor has built a contraption to get to the bottom of the ghost mystery. When the next shift begins, he is able to trap a ghost, but this immediately brings the Doctor to the attention of the Torchwood Institute, who are able to pinpoint his location using CCTV.

The Doctor traces the source and sets off in the Tardis with both Rose and Jackie in tow. They materialise in the middle of the Torchwood Institute. The Doctor emerges to face a group of soldiers and Yvonne Hartman, who give him a round of applause. Yvonne takes the Doctor and Jackie to a laboratory containing a large sphere. The Doctor says it is a Void Ship, which is designed to exist in the gap between parallel universes. They head back upstairs. Rose sneaks out of the Tardis and into the Void Ship laboratory, where she sees a familiar face, Mickey Smith.

Something goes wrong as the Cyber-controlled workers override the system and start another ghost shift. The Doctor traces the source of the override to another area, where he is confronted by an army of Cybermen, who take control of the ghost shift and increase it to 100%. More and more Cybermen start appearing all over the world.

In the laboratory, the sphere begins to open. Mickey stands firm with a large gun, but instead of Cybermen, a group of Daleks appear. The Daleks reject an offer from the Cybermen to form an alliance. The Cybermen warn the Daleks that they have declared war. 'This is not war,' declares the black Dalek. 'This is pest control!'

A group of soldiers appears in the lever room led by Jake, who was last seen in 'The Age of Steel'. Jake says they are able to travel from one universe to another and takes the Doctor back to the parallel Earth, where he is reunited with Pete Tyler.

Pete tells him that his Earth is threatened with catastrophic global warming because of the breach between the two realities. The only way to save both of them is to seal the breach.

They return back to the 'normal' universe. The Doctor walks into the laboratory, where the Daleks are holed up, and a great battle ensues. Mickey touches the Genesis Ark, which primes the device. The Daleks take the Genesis Ark up into the sky above London and thousands of Daleks start to shoot out of it. The Doctor explains that because the Daleks and Cybermen have come through Void, they are both covered in 'Void stuff'. If they can open the Void again, anything covered in this substance will be sucked inside and then the breach can be closed forever.

They open the breach. The Doctor and Rose cling onto two magna-clamps as the Daleks and Cybermen are sucked inside. Rose falls towards the breach, but she is grabbed by Pete who takes her into his universe. The breach seals, leaving the Doctor and Rose separated forever. A few weeks later, Rose starts to hear a voice calling to her. It leads her to a beach in Norway called Bad Wolf Bay, where a projection of the Doctor appears. She tells him she loves him, but before he can reply, the Doctor fades away. Tearful and alone, the Doctor is back in the Tardis, or least he thinks he is. Standing in front of him is a red-haired woman in a wedding dress.

Trivia and facts

The series two finale sees the first time Daleks and the Cybermen had fought each other in the television series, although the two alien races briefly appeared together in the 1989 stage play *Doctor Who: The Ultimate Adventure*. Written by the late Terrance Dicks, the play initially saw Jon Pertwee as the Third Doctor battle a number of foes. The Sixth Doctor Colin Baker took over from Pertwee towards the end of the stage run, with David Banks, who played the Cyberleader in the 1980s playing the Doctor for one performance.

Russell T. Davies' initial outline was entitled 'Army of Ghosts' and based in Cardiff, where the Torchwood Institute had a top floor laboratory in a skyscraper. To keep Rose's fate secret, copies of the script sent to the production team finished with her disappearance in Pete's arms. The Daleks were referred to as 'the Enemy' on rehearsal call sheets to keep their appearance a secret.

While filming her scenes, Freema Agyeman was spotted by the production team who were then thinking about casting the next companion. In order to keep Billie Piper's departure a secret, the team suggested Agyeman audition for a role in the adult spin-off programme Torchwood.

The 'Bad Wolf Bay' scene was filmed on Southerndown Beach on 16 January 2006. While recording, a group of windsurfers wandered into shot and had to be asked to leave. The last scene to be filmed was Catherine Tate's surprise appearance at the end of the final episode. This took place on the Tardis set on the evening of 31 March 2006, while most of the crew were at the series two wrap party.

Season Three

'The Runaway Bride'

Original UK airdate: 25 December 2006
Cast: David Tennant as The Doctor, Catherine Tate as Donna, Sarah Parish as the Empress, Don Gilet as Lance Bennett, Howard Atfield as Geoff Noble, Jacqueline King as Sylvia Noble, Trevor Georges as the Vicar, Glen Wilson as the Taxi Driver, Krystal Archer as Nerys, Rhodri Melir as Rhodri, Zafirah Boateng as the Little Girl and Paul Kasey as Robot Santa
Written by Russell T. Davis
Directed by Euros Lyn
Music by Murray Gold
Produced by Phil Collinson
Filming dates: the main filming block ran from 4 July to 3 August 2006. An extra day's filming took place on 19 October
Running time: 60 minutes
Original UK viewing figures: 9.4 million

Review

With the Tenth Doctor still mourning the loss of Rose and the Christmas Day audience still munching their way through the leftovers, 'The Runaway Bride' is the perfect opportunity for everyone involved to have a bit of a knees-up. The pairing of Catherine Tate and David Tennant might have been controversial at the time, with some fans fearing the comedienne would take the series back to the bad old days of 1980s celebrity cameos, such as Hale and Pace, Ken Dodd and - shudder - Beryl Reid. But Tate is a fine actress, who knows when to milk it for laughs and when to play it straight. Her scene at the end, where Donna tells the Doctor that he needs to find someone, is particularly well done.

The pace of 'The Runaway Bride' is like a Hollywood Screwball comedy, with plenty of set pieces and chases. The CGI effect of the Tardis flying down the motorway, might have aged badly, particularly in a world dominated by high definition television, but it was one of the most ambitious scenes ever mounted by the Doctor Who production team at the time. Sarah Parish also chews the scenery as the Empress of Racnoss, but if ever there was an acting role that did not require any subtlety whatsoever, then it was probably this one.

If there is one thing that feels slightly out of place, then it's the more vengeful side of the Doctor, with the Time Lord standing in judgement over the Empress and her children. It's a chilling moment, in what has been a light-hearted romp, but Russell T. Davies does like his occasional moments of darkness. There are also moments when it's quite obvious that the episode was filmed in the middle of the summer, which it was. But apart from such minor niggles, 'The Runaway Bride' is guaranteed to put a smile on your face, even if you've had one too many servings of granny's sherry trifle.

The story

It should have been the happiest day of Donna Noble's life, but as she walks down the aisle, the bride vanishes in a gaseous swirl. Seconds later, she appears in the Doctor's Tardis, thousands of light-years away from Earth. Donna demands the Doctor return her to the wedding at St. Mary's Church in Chiswick, immediately. They land in central London and Donna gets into a taxi, which is being driven by one of the robot Santa's, last seen in the 'The Christmas Invasion'.

Realising Donna is in danger, the Doctor sets off in the Tardis, in hot pursuit. As the taxi heads onto the motorway, the Tardis pulls alongside the vehicle and Donna jumps onboard. The Doctor takes Donna to the wedding reception, which is in full swing, despite her disappearance. As the party continues, the Doctor realises that Huon particles caused Donna to vanish and re-appear in the Tardis. But the reception is cut short when he sees more robot Santas approach the hotel. Fortunately, he is able to plug his sonic screwdriver into the sound system and destroy them.

The Time Lord traces the signal, which has been controlling the robots, to a spaceship in the sky, where the Empress of the Racnoss is watching. The Doctor, Donna and her fiancé Lance go to the offices of HC Clements, where they first met. They head to the basement, where they find a tunnel that takes them to a laboratory underneath the Thames Flood Barrier. As they enter the laboratory, they discover a large flood chamber, which contains a shaft that has been drilled down to the centre of the Earth. The Empress of the Racnoss then teleports into the chamber and reveals that Lance has been working for her and dosing Donna with Huon particles for the last six months to help free the Empress's children, who are located at the centre of the Earth.

When the Doctor and Donna escape on board the Tardis, the Empress decides to use Lance instead and starts force-feeding him with water dosed with Huon particles. The Tardis returns to the underground chamber, but Donna is captured and ensnared in a giant web, alongside Lance. The Empress removes the Huon particles from both Donna and Lance and sends them down to the bottom of the hole, where they will bring her children back to life. She then cuts Lance loose and he plunges to his death down the hole.

The Doctor saves Donna and uses explosive baubles to blow holes in the wall. Water starts to burst in and pours down the shaft. The Empress teleports back to her spaceship, but it is destroyed in a barrage of tank gunfire, on the orders of Mr Saxon.

With Donna safely returned home, the Doctor offers her a chance to travel with him. She turns down the offer but makes him promise that he will find someone.

Trivia and facts

The readthrough for 'The Runaway Bride' was held at a hotel in Cardiff city centre on 29 June 2006. Catherine Tate was unable to attend because she was working on other projects, so Donna's lines were read by Tennant's then-girlfriend, the actress Sophia Myles. The first proper day of filming was 6 July with the scenes between Tennant and Tate on the helipad atop the IPC Building in central London, which has since been demolished.

The money which flew out of the London cashpoint was fake and especially designed by the production team. The £10 note featured a picture of Tennant in the Ninth Doctor costume, with the legend:

I promise to pay the bearer on demand the sum of ten satsumas

and 'No second chances – I'm that sort of man', which are both quotes from previous year's festive special, 'The Christmas Invasion'.

The £20 note featured producer Phil Collinson and the quote 'There's no point being grown-up if you can't be a little childish sometimes', which is a reference to the first-ever Fourth Doctor story, 'Robot'.

The wedding reception was filmed at the Baverstock Hotel in Merthyr Tydfil, where DJ Mark Haste provided his own equipment. The external scenes were filmed at a different hotel, the New Country House Hotel in Thornhill, near Cardiff.

The church scenes were recorded at St John the Baptist Church on Trinity Street in Cardiff.

'Smith and Jones'

Original UK airdate: 31 March 2007
Cast: David Tennant as The Doctor, Freema Agyeman as Martha Jones, Anne Reid as Florence Finnegan, Roy Marsden as Mr Stoker, Adjoa Andoh as Francine Jones, Gugu Mbatha-Raw as Tish Jones, Reggie Yates as Leo Jones, Trevor Laird as Clive Jones, Kimmi Richards as Annalise, Ben Righton as Morgenstein, Vineeta Rishi as Julia Swales, Paul Kasey as the Judoon Captain and Nicholas Briggs as the voice of the Judoon
Written by Russell T. Davies
Directed by Charles Palmer
Music by Murray Gold
Produced by Phil Collinson
Filming dates: the main production ran from 8 August to 25 August 2006. There were additional filming days on 12/13 September, 2 October, 13 October, 7 November 2006 and 17 January 2007
Running time: 44 minutes
Original UK viewing figures: 8.7 million

Review

When *Doctor Who* returned to British screens in 2004, critics and viewers were unanimous in their praise of Billie Piper, who was credited as a big factor in the revived show's success. By the time series three was transmitted, the general public had accepted the regeneration of the leading man, but there were big questions about whether the show would remain as popular with a new companion as well.

In many ways, 'Smith & Jones' is the revived Doctor Who's 'difficult second album', which ran the risk of playing it safe by rehashing a proven formula or trying something new, which could have sent millions of viewers to the remote and whatever was being shown on ITV at the time. Smith & Jones is actually a bit of both. It's the kind of fast-paced adventure that viewers knew and loved, with plenty of dashing about for the Tenth Doctor and the introduction of another alien race, the Judoon, who were an instant hit.

But there are also important changes, with a different dynamic between the Doctor and his new companion, Martha Jones. Freema Agyeman makes an immediate impact as the wide-eyed, feisty and brave trainee doctor. If the production team were bracing themselves for a backlash, then they did not have to worry. Martha Jones proved to be a big success and still is popular with fans to this day, having also transitioned over to Torchwood along the way.

It's a shame the 'vampire' Plasmavore with the drinking straw feels a little half-baked, although Anne Reid certainly seems to make the most of what little screen time she has. Mind you, Doctor Who has always had a difficult relationship with bloodsuckers, as anyone who has seen the First Doctor take on Dracula and Frankenstein in the 1965 adventure 'The Chase' will testify.

The story

Medical student Martha Jones is walking to work one day at the Royal Hope Hospital when she encounters the Doctor, who for some unknown reason takes his tie off in front of her. When she arrives at the hospital and starts doing rounds of the hospital ward, she meets the Doctor again, who is a patient at the hospital, but he does not recognise her at all.

It starts raining outside the hospital, but instead of falling to the ground, the raindrops are going upwards into the sky. Moments later, the hospital building starts to shake, and the sky turns dark outside. Martha realises the building is now on the moon. As patients start to panic, the Doctor appears and takes Martha onto a balcony, where he shows her that there is now a forcefield around the hospital. They look on as a series of spaceships land next to the building at which point, out march an intergalactic space force known as the Judoon.

As the Judoon enter the hospital and start scanning everyone in it, an old lady called Florence is using a straw to drink the blood of consultant, Mr Stoker. The Doctor quickly realises that Florence is a Plasmavore and is assimilating his blood, so when she is scanned by the Judoon she will appear as human. The Doctor heads down to the MRI room, where he finds Florence interfering with the scanner. The Plasmavore is planning to use the scanner to fry the brains of every living being within 250,000 miles of the moon. The Judoon and Martha burst into the room and find the Doctor on the floor, apparently dead. The Judoon then scan Florence, who registers as non-human because she has drunk the Doctor's blood.

Florence activates the scanner, but the Judoon then execute her and withdraw to their spaceships. Martha resuscitates the Doctor, who is able to deactivate the scanner. The hospital then returns back to its original site in London.

Later, Martha spots the Doctor and the Tardis in an alleyway. He proves he can travel in time by going back to see her that morning, as she walked to work. They then depart for a new set of adventures.

Trivia and facts

Showrunner Russell T. Davies originally envisaged Martha as a 16-year old schoolgirl and then a Victorian maid, but he ditched both ideas after discussing them with BBC Drama Commissioner Jane Tranter. Freema Agyeman performed her audition for the role of Martha Jones with David Tennant, at producer Phil Collinson's flat on 15 February 2006. When she arrived in Cardiff for the audition, she found a note from Tennant at her hotel, which read: 'Sorry for all the cloak and dagger stuff, it's going to be fine. Relax and have a good time.'

In the previous series, Agyeman had played Adeola in 'Army of Ghosts', and so there was a line in the script, explaining that she was Martha's cousin. In the BBC press release announcing her appointment on 5 July 2006, Russell T. Davies said:

> The search for a new companion had been underway for some time when I first saw Freema Agyeman: she had come in to audition for the part of Adeola in series two. Watching her during filming, confirmed what an exciting new talent she was. So, under cover of darkness, we called her back in to audition with David for the role of the new companion. It was an immediate and sensational combination, and her range, presence and charm blew us all away.

In one early draft of 'Smith and Jones', the Doctor and Martha fled from the Judoon by hijacking a window cleaner's cradle and heading down the outside of the building. While this idea was not used in 'Smith and Jones', it would later appear in the series four opener 'Partners in Crime'.

The disused School of Sciences at the University of Glamorgan at Pontypridd and Singleton Hospital in Swansea were both used to film the interior and exterior hospital scenes. The scenes in the hospital kitchen were actually recorded in the real staff kitchen at Upper Boat Studios, where the production team of Doctor Who was based.

The Shakespeare Code

Original UK airdate: 7 April 2007
Cast: David Tennant as The Doctor, Freema Agyeman as Martha Jones, Dean

Lennox Kelly as Shakespeare, Christine Cole as Lilith, Sam Marks as Wiggins, Amanda Lawrence as Doomfinger, Linda Clark as Bloodtide, Jalaal Hartley as Dick, David Westhead as Kempe, Andree Bernard as Dolly Bailey, Chris Larkin as Lynley, Stephen Marcus as the Jailer, Matt King as Peter Streete, Robert Demeger as the Preacher and Angela Presence as Queen Elizabeth
Written by Gareth Roberts
Directed by Charles Palmer
Music by Murray Gold
Produced by Phil Collinson
Filming dates: the main production ran from 23 August to 15 September 2006, with an additional day's filming on 2 and 13 October
Running time: 45 minutes
Original UK viewing figures: 7.2 million

Review

As anyone who has endured the agony of endless English Literature A-Level classes will tell you, William Shakespeare is quite dull, especially in the wrong hands.

Fortunately, Russell T. Davies had the good sense to bring in one of the wittiest and sharpest minds to ever write Doctor Who, Gareth Roberts. His 1995 novel *The Romance of Crime* is one of the finest Fourth Doctor stories never to make it to the television screen, although Big Finish have produced an excellent audio version, which is well worth hunting down.

Roberts' knowledge and love of Shakespeare are all too evident in a script that finally manages to makes Shakespeare cool again by using the real-life mystery about the missing sequel to *Love Labour's Lost*. The gag about '57 academics punching the air' might raise a few eyebrows, but it proves that Roberts knows his subject matter, cleverly referencing the Bard's Sonnet '57', where the poet expresses his love for a young man. And getting Dean Lennox Kelly to play the Bard as a preening rock star might not please your stuffy English Literature teacher, but it's an inspired choice. Chuck in a trio of scheming witches and you have a caper of which even Shakespeare himself would be proud.

There are also hints that the Doctor's relationship with Martha might not be quite as perfect as the one he enjoyed with Rose Tyler. 'The Shakespeare Code' is remarkably assured, with a nod to *Shakespeare in Love* at the end with a fuming Queen Elizabeth. Although viewers would have to wait to the 50th anniversary special, 'The Day of the Doctor' to find out why she might have a grudge to bear against the Tenth Doctor.

The story

The Doctor and Martha land in Southwark in 1599, near the Globe Theatre, where William Shakespeare's plays are performed every night. They watch a performance of *Love's Labour's Lost* and then at the end, Shakespeare himself appears on stage and announces a sequel, *Love Labour's Won*. But he is being secretly controlled by an evil witch, called Lilith.

Afterwards, the Doctor and Martha visit Shakespeare in the Elephant, where the legendary playwright takes a shine to Martha. But they are interrupted by the Master of the Revels, Lynley, who forbids any performance of *Love's Labour Won*. As Lynley returns to his office, he is accosted by Lilith, who plucks a piece of his hair and uses it to take possess his body and make his lungs fill with water and drown. The Doctor says the death is the work of witchcraft. Lilith then makes Shakespeare finish *Love's Labour Won*. The Doctor and Martha rush in, but Lilith flies off on a broomstick.

The following day, the Doctor, Martha and Shakespeare return to the globe. The playwright hands the finished script to actors Dick and Kempe. As they rehearse the closing speech, a ghostly apparition appears briefly in front of them. The Doctor, Martha and Shakespeare then head to Bedlam hospital, where they meet the architect who designed the Globe Theatre, Peter Streete, who informs them that the witches made him build the Globe to their design. However, they are interrupted by another witch, who teleports into the cell and kills Streete before he can tell anymore. The Doctor realises the witches are Carrionites and have designed the Globe to be a psychic energy converter, which will be unleashed by a secret code buried in the *Loves Labour Won* script.

Shakespeare rushes to the Globe and tries to stop the play's performance, but Doomfinger uses a puppet to knock him unconscious. As Dick starts to perform Love's Labour Won, a portal opens above the stage, and thousands of screaming witches start to fly through. The Doctor realises the portal can be closed by speaking the correct sequence of words. Shakespeare starts to improvise a speech but gets stuck until Martha cries out 'Expelliarmus!'. The portal closes and the witches are trapped in their own crystal ball.

The following day, the Doctor and Martha say goodbye to Shakespeare, but they are interrupted by the arrival of Queen Elizabeth, who announces the Doctor is her sworn enemy. The Doctor and Martha then run back to the Tardis, which dematerialises as the Queens' guards start firing arrows.

Trivia and facts

Russell T. Davies' brief to writer Gareth Roberts was a one-word email, which said simply 'Shakespeare'. Fortunately, Roberts was soon able to come up with a strong hook for the story – *Love's Labour Won*, a Shakespeare play which is mentioned in both Francis Mere's guidebook Palladis Tamia in 1598 and another catalogue in 1603, but no manuscript was ever found. Davies told *Doctor Who Confidential*:

> One of the first things he said was 'Did you know there was actually a lost play of Shakespeare's?' and that was it Suddenly, you felt the whole story click into place.

'*The Shakespeare Code*' became one of the revitalised show's most ambitious productions to date, with filming in Coventry, Warwick and the Globe Theatre in London. Ford's Hospital in Greyfriars Lane, Coventry and the Lord Leicester Hospital, High Street, Warwick, provided some suitably historical backdrops.

The Doctor Who team starting filming at the Globe for three nights, starting on 31 August 2006. It was the first time a drama had been allowed to film at the venue, and the production team had to wait until 10 pm each night when the last performance ended before setting up inside.

The scenes in Bedlam were filmed in the basement of Newport Indoor Market, while everything else was recreated at the Upper Boat Studios. For a long time, the episode title was going to be 'Love Labour's Won'. Another title – 'Theatre of Death'– was also considered, before the production team opted for 'The Shakespeare Code' in homage to Dan Brown's 2003 best-selling novel, The Da Vinci Code.

'Gridlock'

Original UK airdate: 14 April 2007
Cast: David Tennant as The Doctor, Freema Agyeman as Martha Jones, Ardal O'Hanlon as Brannigan, Anna Hope as Novice Hame, Travis Oliver as Milo, Lenora Crichlow as Cheen, Jennifer Hennessy as Valerie, Bridget Turner as Alice, Georgine Anderson as May, Simon Pearsell as Whitey, Daisy Lewis as Javit, Nicholas Boulton as the Businessman, Erika Macleod as Sally Calypso, Judy Norman as Ma, Graham Padden as Pa, Lucy Davenport as Pale Woman and Struan Rodger as the Face of Boe
Written by Russell T. Davies
Directed by Richard Clark
Music by Murray Gold
Produced by Phil Collinson
Filming dates: the main production ran from 18 September to 2 October 2006, with additional filming days on 18 October and 7 November
Running time: 44 minutes
Original UK viewing figures: 8.4 million

Review

While 'Gridlock' at times feels like *Bladerunner* on a budget, there's a strong argument for saying this is one of Russell T. Davies' strongest and most underrated *Doctor Who* scripts. The idea of the human race trapped on an enclosed motorway traffic jam for years and years, desperately trying to make their way to the fast lane, where they will meet their doom is a brilliant science fiction concept in itself. Talk about big ideas. If ever there was a perfect metaphor for the futility of being a commuter, then it is 'Gridlock'.

And the sight of the drivers singing hymns as they dream of a better life is so incredibly poignant that you can overlook the fact that each car is clearly the same set, just re-dressed for different characters. If the sight of the motorists finally heading for freedom does not move you, then you may need to consult a medical practitioner as soon as possible.

The return of the Macra, who had not been seen in Doctor Who since 1967's 'The Macra Terror' is a nice touch. Admittedly, the villainous crabs are not in 'Gridlock' for long, but it's good to see them back. If there's one flaw, it's the sudden arrival of Novice Hame and the massive leap in logic about how the Face of Boe engineered the traffic jam to save the residents of New New York and how the Doctor is able to free them all with relative ease.

But above all, the episode belongs to David Tennant, who takes the character of the Tenth Doctor to new levels. The fire of fury of the Doctor as his companion is kidnapped shows this incarnation of the Time Lord is not to be trifled with, and the scene where the Doctor finally admits to Martha that his homeworld of Gallifrey and all his people are gone is incredibly moving and proves why Tennant was born to play the role.

The story

The Doctor takes Martha on another trip, but this time they head to the future and New New York, which was last seen in 'New Earth'. The Tardis lands in an alleyway, where street vendors sell chemical patches to help people alter their moods – like Happy, Anger and Mellow. Martha is then kidnapped by a couple, Milo and Cheen, who explain that Cheen is pregnant and that they needed three adult passengers with them to use the fast lane on the motorway. They are heading to Brooklyn, where the air is cleaner. Brooklyn is only ten miles away, but the journey will take around six years.

The Doctor heads to the motorway, determined to rescue Martha. He is picked up by a friendly cat-person called Brannigan and his wife, Valerie, who have been stuck on the motorway for twelve years. The Doctor uses Brannigan's radio to contact the police, but he is put on hold. Brannigan calls another car, which is driven by the Cassini Sisters. They give him the number of the car that took Martha.

Milo, Cheen and Martha head down to the fast track, where the air is thick with exhaust fumes. The Doctor leaves Brannigan's car and starts to jump down from one car to another, in an attempt to reach the fast lane. As he gets lower and lower into the depths of the motorway, he sees the claws of a giant crab, better known as the Macra.

Novice Hame appears in Brannigan's car, looking for the Doctor. She has been sent to find him by the Face of Boe, who has detected his arrival. She eventually catches up with him, who informs him the Face of Boe is dying. Novice Hame transports him back to the Senate building, which is littered with skeletons.

She explains that a virus wiped out the entire population, but the Face of Boe sealed the motorway using his own life force to protect people from the virus. Using the remainder of his life force, the Doctor is able to open up the motorway ceiling, which allows everyone stuck in their cars – including Milo,

Cheen and Martha - to fly away to safety. The Face of Boe then reveals his final secret, telling the Doctor 'You are not alone', before passing away.

Trivia and facts

Filming started on 18 September 2006 after the bulk of 'The Shakespeare Code' was in the can. The Temple of Peace at the Welsh Centre for International Affairs in College Road, Cardiff, was used to record the Darkened Temple scenes.

One main interior car set was built for at Upper Boat Studios and then redecorated for different scenes and characters.

The Sally Calypso character is a homage to the 2000AD comic strip Halo Jones, which featured a similar character called Swifty Frisko. The hymn sung by the travellers on the motorway is 'The Old Rugged Cross', which was written in 1912 by the evangelist George Bennard. The cast wore hidden earpieces so that they could hear a recording of the song being played back in the scenes. Composer Murray Gold did write a wordless hymn with choir voices for the end of the episode, but it was later decided by the production team to use the hymn 'Abide With Me', which was composed by Henry Lyte in 1847.

The final day of filming was 2 October 2006, which did not feature either Tennant or Agyeman, who were out on location filming 'Smith and Jones'. The Face of Boe's dialogue was changed in post-production after filming had finished, referring to the Doctor as an 'old friend' because Russell T. Davies decided to imply that he was actually Captain Jack Harkness, which would be properly revealed later in the series. Davies had already revealed the secret in his 'Meet The Doctor' feature in Panini's Doctor Who Annual 2006, which was published in August 2005. The feature states:

> The artwork shows two races clashing, one metal, one flesh, and a solitary survivor walking from the wreckage. Solitary? Perhaps not. Under this figure, a phrase has been scratched in the stone, which translates as 'you are not alone...'

'Daleks in Manhattan/Evolution of the Daleks'

Original UK airdate: 21/28 April 2007
Cast: David Tennant as The Doctor, Freema Agyeman as Martha Jones, Miranda Raison as Tallulah, Ryan Carnes as Laszlo, Hugh Quarshie as Solomon, Andrew Garfield as Frank, Eric Loren as Mr Diagoras/Dalek Sec, Flik Swan as Myrna, Alexis Caley as Lois, Earl Perkins as Man #1, Peter Brooke as Man #2, Ian Porter as Foreman/Hybrid, Joe Montana as Worker #1, Stewart Alexander as Worker #2, Mel Taylor as Dock Worker, Paul Kasey as Hero Pig Man, Barnaby Edwards, Nicholas Pegg, Anthony Spargo and David Hankinson as Dalek operators, and Nicholas Briggs as the voice of the Daleks
Written by Helen Raynor
Directed by James Strong
Music by Murray Gold

Produced by Phil Collinson
Filming dates: the main production ran from 13 October to 23 November 2006, with additional filming days on 5/8 December
Running time: 46/46 minutes
Original UK viewing figures: 6.6/6.9 million

Review

What the *Doctor Who* team might have lacked in terms of money, they frequently made up for with jaw-dropping ingenuity, being able to find locations within spitting distance of their Cardiff base that could double for almost anything. It says a lot about the production team's brilliance that the number of times this resourcefulness failed them were few and far between. Unfortunately '*Daleks in Manhattan/Evolution of the Daleks*' is one of those times.

While the idea of the Daleks using the construction of the Empire State Building in New York for their own, nefarious ends is a good idea in itself, the wheels fall off this story within minutes of the first episode starting and it never fully recovers. It's quite obvious that nobody is really in New York, despite the best efforts to recreate the 1930s shanty town Hooverville and some plate shots of its actual skyline. The pig men stray dangerously close to the dodgy rubber costumes of the 1970s and 1980s. Quite why the Daleks would bother with creating them in the first place is another mystery as it's already fairly well-established that the Daleks can brainwash and robotise humans. Maybe, they had a 1950s horror movie night in Skaro and one of them went 'we should try that sometime!'. Thank Davros that it never happened again.

The story itself does not work either. Doctor Who is always noted for bonkers plots and general silliness, but this two-parter feels like a step too far, even for a show like this. For once, the Doctor's victory is never really in doubt, nor the fact that one of the Daleks will make it out alive and then live to fight another day. If you're looking for a contender for the one story of the season everyone would rather forget about, then it's this one.

The story

It's 1930, and as America enters the Great Depression, something strange is happening in the sewers beneath the streets of New York. A young actress, Tallulah, is visited by her boyfriend, Laszlo in her dressing room, just before she is due to go on stage and sing. After she leaves, Laszlo hears a grunting sound and decides to investigate. He wanders deep into the heart of the backstage area and is attacked by a pig-like creature.

The Tardis materialises at the bottom of the Statue of Liberty on Liberty Island. As they look out on the New York skyline, Martha picks up a newspaper, which has the headline 'Hooverville Mystery Deepens'. They visit Hooverville, a shantytown in the middle of Central Park, which is full of the homeless and destitute. The Doctor and Martha meet a man called Solomon, who is trying his

51

best to keep the peace amongst its residents.

Meanwhile at the Empire State Building, which is still under construction, a Mafia-like boss called Mr Diagoras is ordering his men to work faster. When the foreman refuses, a Dalek and two pig slaves appear and drag him off for experimentation.

Diagoras then heads to Hooverville and appeals for more volunteers. He sends Solomon, the Doctor, Martha and a young man called Frank down to the sewers, where they discover some green jellyfish-like creatures. The Daleks summon Diagoras to the laboratory in the basement of the Empire State Building, where pig slaves grab him. Down in the sewers, the Doctor, Martha, Solomon and Frank meet more pig slaves. They escape up a ladder into the theatre that was seen earlier and meet Tallulah.

She explains to them that her boyfriend Laszlo went missing two weeks ago, but even though he has vanished, someone keeps leaving a rose in her dressing room every night. The Doctor and Tallulah head back into the sewers and they find a pig slave cowering in the darkness. Enter Laszlo, who has been experimented upon by the Daleks. The Time Lord, Martha and Frank head for the Daleks' laboratory. The lead Dalek – Dalek Sec - is in the 'final stages of evolution'. They look on in horror as its casing opens and the body of Diagoras steps out, except he has a Dalek head. 'I am Dalek in human form,' he announces. They manage to escape and they race back to Hooverville. The Doctor warns Solomon that the Daleks will attack the settlement, but it is too late. Hooverville is soon under attack from pig slaves and Daleks, who surround them.

The Doctor offers to let the Daleks exterminate him if they will spare everyone, but Sec intervenes and says the Time Lord must live. The metal monsters then lead him away. Back in the laboratory, Sec explains that they will use the Empire State Building as an energy conductor to splice its DNA into an army of humans. Sec asks the Doctor for help to make this new race become even more human.

The Doctor and Sec work together, but the other Daleks turn against their leader and alter the gene feed to the new race and make it '100% Dalek'. The Doctor and Laszlo head up to the top of the building, where they find Martha and Tallulah.

The Doctor realises he must remove the Dalekanium plates on the mast before gamma radiation strikes. But lightning strikes the mast and passes through the Doctor. In the laboratory, the converted humans wake up and the Daleks order them to invade Manhattan. When the Doctor recovers, he says he must face the converted humans in the theatre.

Once they arrive, the Daleks appear on stage with Sec, who is now their prisoner. They order the humans to kill the Doctor, but he explains that they received some Time Lord DNA when he was struck on the mast, and they turn their fire against the Daleks. Two of the Daleks are destroyed, but the remaining one – Caan – is able to escape using an emergency temporal shift.

Trivia and facts

Russell T. Davies' shopping list to writer Helen Raynor for this two-parter included New York, 1930s, pig men, sewers, showgirls and the Daleks. Early versions of the script did contain pig men dressed in 1930s suits and a steam-driven Dalek, which had been patched up with wood after arriving in New York. The story also sees the programme's first official recording in the USA. A small crew, including director James Houghton, producer Phil Collinson, visual effects supervisor Dave Houghton and a cameraman flew out to New York for three days in October 2006 to record various plate shots of the city's skyline and the Statue of Liberty.

These images were then mixed with footage recorded in and around Cardiff for the final episode. For example, the scene where the Doctor and Martha land at the base of the Statue of Liberty, was mostly filmed by a stone wall at Penarth Leisure Centre with Tennant and Agyeman looking out on a football pitch. The view of New York was added in later. Bute Park in the centre of Cardiff was transformed into Hooverville for the production with plate shots filmed in Central Park used for the skyline. The Park and Dare Theatre in Treorchy, which was built in 1913 was used for all the stage scenes, while the dressing room and basement scenes were all shot at Headlands School in Penarth.

At the start of 'Daleks in Manhattan', the music heard in the theatre is 'Happy Days Are Here Again' by Milton Ager and Jack Yellen, and originally heard in the 1930 musical Chasing Rainbows. The arrival of the Tardis was backed by George Gershwin's 'Rhapsody in Blue', and as the Doctor and Martha walk through Central Park, Irving Berlin's 1929 song 'Putting' on the Ritz' was also used.

'The Lazarus Experiment'

Original UK airdate: 5 May 2007
Cast: David Tennant as The Doctor, Freema Agyeman as Martha Jones, Gugu Mbatha-Raw as Tish Jones, Reggie Yates as Leo Jones, Adjoa Andoh as Francine Jones, Mark Gatiss as Lazarus, Thelma Barlow as Lady Thaw, Lucy O'Connell as Olive Woman and Bertie Carvel as the Mysterious Man
Written by Stephen Greenhorn
Directed by Richard Clark
Music by Murray Gold
Produced by Phil Collinson
Filming dates: the main production ran from 3 October to 19 October 2006, with an additional filming day on 7 November
Running time: 43 minutes
Original UK viewing figures: 7.1 million

Review

Despite featuring quite prominently in the third series teaser trailer, 'The Lazarus Experiment' frequently gets overlooked in a season full of bigger and more revered episodes. While it might lack the emotional drama of 'Human

Nature' or the originality of 'Blink', there is still a lot to enjoy in 'The Lazarus Experiment'. It is a solid and well-written tale, using the well-worn concept of a mad scientist stepping into a machine, which (quelle surprise) turns him into a monster. It might not be as creepy as Jeff Goldblum in *The Fly*, or anything else starring the Goldblum for that matter, but it's still entertaining to watch.

It also features Mark Gatiss in a rare role that does not require him to be a bumbling General or Sherlock Holmes' older brother. His scenes with David Tennant in the cathedral, however brief, are a timely reminder that he is a fine actor when the moment demands it. Although the script must have been a 'bus man's holiday' for the horror movie aficionado.

It also stands up to multiple viewings with some interesting references to the series' 'big bad' Harold Saxon sprinkled in for good measure. The CGI monster might not look too scary in a world where high-definition creatures are indistinguishable from the real thing but there are a lot of explosions and chase sequences, and such things never did the Marvel Cinematic Universe any harm. 'The Lazarus Experiment' is neither big nor clever, but it does exactly what is expected of it.

The story

The Doctor returns Martha back to her own time, where she sees her sister on the television news with the elderly Professor Richard Lazarus. Lazarus announces he has built a device which will 'change what it means to be human'. Later that day and dressed in black tie, the Doctor and Martha attend a lavish party at Lazarus Laboratories. Martha's sister, brother Leo and mother, Francine are also at the event.

Lazarus introduces himself and then steps inside a large capsule. The capsule soon overloads, and the Doctor is forced to unplug it, but to everyone's amazement, the Professor emerges and is now 40 years younger. Lazarus returns to his office with his elderly partner, Lady Thaw. They argue and Lady Thaw threatens to have Mr Saxon withdraw the project's funding. But Lazarus collapses and starts to turn into a hideous creature. He then kills her. Moments later, Lazarus re-appears in human form at the reception. He starts flirting with Tish, but Martha warns her sister to get away from him as he starts to transform back again into a huge scorpion-like monster.

The monster chases the Doctor, Martha and Tish through the building. Eventually, it follows the Doctor into a laboratory, where he sets off an explosion. The Time Lord then runs into Martha, and they step inside the capsule. The monster activates the capsule, but the Doctor has reversed the polarity, which causes the monster to transform back into the human Lazarus. An ambulance takes Lazarus away, but it soon crashes. The Doctor and Martha investigate and find his body is missing.

They head off to Southwark Cathedral and find the still-human Lazarus cowering on the floor inside. The Doctor orders Martha to entice Lazarus up to the bell tower at the top of the cathedral. The Time Lord then augments the cathedral organ with his sonic screwdriver. As the Doctor starts to play the organ, the noise causes the monster to fall from the bell tower and onto the floor below. Lazarus reverts into an old man and dies. The Doctor and Martha then depart. As the Tardis dematerialises, Francine leaves a message on her answering machine. 'This information comes from Harold Saxon himself. You're not safe,' she warns her daughter.

Trivia and facts

Showrunner Russell T. Davies' original brief to writer Stephen Greenhorn was 'mad scientist, present-day'. Its working title was 'The Madness of Professor Lazarus' but was later changed to 'The Lazarus Experiment'. More than half-way through the writing process, Davis also asked Greenhorn to make Harold Saxon the mysterious sponsor of Lazarus Laboratories, setting up the return of the Master for later in the series.

At the tone meeting for 'The Lazarus Experiment', which was recorded alongside 'Gridlock', Davies told the production team that the starting point/style should be a Marvel comic. Wells Cathedral stood in for Southwark Cathedral, with the crew based at the EMI Sports and Social Club in Chamberlain Street. At the time, the Wells Journal reported that David Tennant had been spotted by fans in the city's branch of Starbucks enjoying a cup of strong coffee before filming. Tennant told Doctor Who Confidential:

I'm very glad we got to go there because it's such a stunning location. You've got these incredible vaulted ceilings and the great organ loft, which was so much part of what we needed.

Organist David Bednall performed all the close-ups of the Doctor's hands when he played the cathedral organ in the story. The reception scenes were all filmed in the central lobby at the Senedd, which is the home of the Welsh National Assembly and in Cardiff Bay. Other scenes were filmed at the lobby of the Cardiff National Museum in the city centre.

'42'

Original UK airdate: 19 May 2007
Cast: David Tennant as The Doctor, Freema Agyeman as Martha Jones, Michelle Collins as Kath McDonnell, Adjoa Andoh as Francine Jones, William Ash as Riley Vashtee, Anthony Flanagan as Orin Scannell, Matthew Chamber as Hal Korwin, Gary Powell as Dev Ashton, Vinette Robinson as Abi Lerner, Rebecca Oldfield as Erina Lessak and Elize Du Toit as the Sinister Woman
Written by Chris Chibnall
Directed by Graeme Harper
Music by Murray Gold
Produced by Phil Collinson
Filming dates: the main production ran from 15 January to 9 February 2007, with

additional filming days on 20 February, 1/6 and 13 March
Running time: 45 minutes
Original UK viewing figures: 7.4 million

Review

The third series of Doctor Who was notable for a powerhouse script by a future showrunner, which gave fans hope that their beloved programme would have a long and rich future. But that was 'Blink', which sprung from the fertile mind of Steven Moffat, and more on that later. '42' was also written by another future showrunner, Chris Chibnall and it is fair to say that his Doctor Who debut did not get the same reception that 'Blink' received.

More than a decade on, two things come to mind about '42'. Firstly, the real-time format might have been popular at the time, thanks to the success of '24' and the mighty Jack Bauer, but it swiftly gets forgotten about in this story. Perhaps having a clock counting down on the screen during the episode might have helped, but in a show where danger is always a split second away and will get resolved by the end of the episode anyway, putting a 42-minute limit on the story feels unnecessary.

Instead, '42' is a workman-like tale of yet another crew onboard an industrial spaceship under threat from an alien menace. The twist, that the Doctor becomes possessed, is a good one, but by plonking it in the middle of the season, you do figure out that everything will be all right in the end. There are nods to the show's future direction under Chibnall with an explanation at the end that the aliens are not really the bad guys and trying to reclaim what has been stolen from them, which feels like a theme straight from the Thirteenth Doctor era. It might not have the originality or flair of 'Blink', but very few Doctor Who stories do. It's nowhere near as dire as 'Daleks in Manhattan', but '42' will be on few fan's all-time favourite lists.

The story

The Tardis receives a distress signal, and when they arrive on the spaceship, the Doctor and Martha find that in 42 minutes, the ship will crash into the sun. The ship's engines have been sabotaged by one of the crew. The Doctor asks about auxiliary engines but is told by Kath McDonnell they are at the front of the ship, and in order to get to them, someone needs to pass through 29 deadlocked and password-protected doors. Martha and one of the crew, Vashtee head off to open the doors.

Up in the medical bay, Kath's husband Korwin is suffering from an infection, which is causing his body temperature to rise.

Martha and Vashtee pass through the first two doors with ease. Up in the medical bay, Korwin wakes up from sedation and starts yelling 'Burn with me!'. He then opens his eyes and vaporises crew member Lerner with a blinding glare.

Korwin then escapes, dons a welding helmet and starts killing other crew members, before infecting another colleague, Ashton. The possessed Ashton then dons a welding mask and catches up with Martha and Vashtee. They hide from him in an escape pod, but she jettisons it, and Martha and Vashtee float off in the pod, towards the sun.

The Doctor performs a spacewalk to recover the pod but gets infected with the sun. He also learns that the ship has been mining the sun's surface for fuel and took its heart. The sun is now trying to recover its lost parts. The infected Doctor tells Martha he must be put in a stasis chamber and frozen, or the infection will force him to kill her. Martha starts to freeze the doctor, but the power is cut by Korwin. The Doctor tells Martha to vent the engines and dump the fuel. They do so and the engines start working again, allowing the ship to pull away from the sun.

In the Tardis, Martha calls her mother, Francine. It's election day in England, and she wants her daughter to come around. But she is not alone. Harold Saxon's agents are listening in.

Trivia and facts

The original brief given by Russell T. Davies to Chris Chibnall included a spaceship, glowing eyes and a spacewalk. Having submitted his story outline, Chibnall fell down the stairs at home and ended up taking a conference call from Davis and Julie Gardner flat on his back, where they proposed the idea of setting the whole story in real-time. Davies also asked the future *Doctor Who* showrunner to add in some new material with Martha's mother and a sinister agent of Mr Saxon, who was also added at short notice into the previous story, 'The Lazarus Experiment'.

Another late change to the script saw the Doctor giving Martha a key to the Tardis, at the behest of Davies to set up his scripts for the series finale 'The Sound of Drums' and 'Last of the Time Lords'. At the script readthrough for '42', the Doctor's lines were read by script editor and former actor Gary Russell, because Tennant had lost his voice.

A disused paper mill in Caldicot, which was owned by the St Regis Paper Company, was used for the main corridor and engineering scenes onboard the spaceship, which was originally called the SS Icarus in Chibnall's script. The name of the spaceship was changed to SS Pentallian after the production team became aware of a new science fiction movie called Sunshine, in which the crew of a spaceship called the Icarus II had to ignite a dying sun.

And the spacesuit worn by Tennant in this episode was the same as the one used in the previous year's story 'The Impossible Planet/The Satan Pit'. Vinette Robinson would go on to play Rosa Parks in the 2018 *Doctor Who* story 'Rosa', opposite Jodie Whittaker as The Doctor.

'Human Nature/Family of Blood'

Original UK airdate: 26 May/2 June 2007

Cast: David Tennant as The Doctor, Freema Agyeman as Martha Jones, Jessica Hynes as Joan Redfern, Rebekah Staton as Jenny, Thomas Sangster as Tim Latimer,

Harry Lloyd as Baines, Tony Palmer as Hutchinson, Gerard Horan as Clark, Lauren Wilson as Lucy Cartwright, Pip Torrens as Rocastle, Matthew White as Phillips, Derek Smith as the Doorman, Peter Bourke as Mr Chambers and Sophie Turner as the Vicar
Written by Paul Cornell
Directed by Charles Palmer
Music by Murray Gold
Produced by Susie Liggat
Filming dates: the main production ran from 27 November to 15 December 2006. There was then a break for Christmas and work resumed on 3 January and continued until 11 January 2007, with additional filming days on 17 January, 5 and 23 February
Running time: 45/42 minutes
Original UK viewing figures: 7.7/7.2 million

Review

The 1990s were lean times for *Doctor Who*. With the programme off the air and seemingly never coming back, fans had to make do with the Virgin *New Adventure* book series, which took the Time Lord on new and sometimes baffling adventures. Paul Cornell's 1995 novel 'Human Nature' was one of the most popular books in the range and Russell T. Davies' decision to adapt it for the Tenth Doctor's era proved to be one of the showrunner's smartest decisions.

Not only was it an original idea, but it also allowed David Tennant to stretch his acting chops even further as the teacher John Smith. No disrespect to Sylvester McCoy, but the prospect of the Seventh Doctor breaking down in front of Joan Redfern is nowhere near as enticing. It also raises brave questions about the Doctor's character. He might be the hero of our tale, but given all the sacrifices and loneliness, would anyone want to choose that kind of lifestyle? What kind of person never assumes they will fall in love? The Doctor might look human, but in many ways, he is more alien than any of the foes he has faced.

The period setting and the use of so many stunning buildings, including those at Saint Fagans' National Museum of History give the production an extra richness. The World War One scenes at the end look particularly impressive and Martha Jones also gets a large slice of the action. Over the years, a lot of praise has been heaped upon David Tennant for this portrayal of the Doctor, and rightly so, but Freema Agyeman's performance, particularly in 'Human Nature/Family of Blood' is particularly noteworthy. This is Martha Jones' story, as much as it is the Doctor's.

The story

The Doctor and Martha are being pursued through time and space by a group of aliens known as the Family of Blood, who want the Time Lord's life force to keep themselves alive. The Doctor knows the Family has a limited lifespan, so uses the Tardis's chameleon circuit to turn himself into a human being until they die out.

The Tardis lands in 1913, and he takes on the persona of teacher John Smith, with Martha acting as a maid at Farringham School for Boys. All the Doctor's knowledge and personality have been transferred into a fob watch, which sits on the teacher's mantlepiece. The shy and clumsy John has no idea who he really is, but faint memories start to seep through whenever he is dreaming.

The school nurse, Joan Redfern, takes a shine to John Smith and suggests he ask her to the forthcoming dance at the village hall. But the Family have tracked the Tardis to Earth and land outside the village. They take over the bodies of several people, including one of the pupils at the school, Jeremy Baines. Another pupil, Tim Latimer, has psychic abilities and starts to hear the fob watch calling him. He sneaks into the teacher's room one day and takes it. While out walking with Joan, John sees a piano being hoisted into the upper floor of the building. Sensing danger is imminent, he grabs a cricket ball and throws it at the rope, saving a baby from certain death.

Suddenly emboldened, he asks Joan to the dance, and she agrees. Meanwhile, the aliens have also possessed a farmer called Clark, a little girl called Lucy and another maid at the school, Jenny. When Martha realises that Jenny is no longer herself, she races off to the village hall dance and tries to tell John who he really is. But the dance is interrupted by the aliens' arrival, who now know the Doctor has taken human form. Baines tells John to turn back into the Doctor and they hold guns to the heads of both Martha and Joan. The frightened teacher must decide between his friend and his lover.

Fortunately, Martha overpowers Jenny and takes her weapon. She then orders the rest of the aliens to lower their weapons and everyone escapes. John and Joan run back to the school, where the teacher sounds the alarm as the aliens and their army of scarecrows approach. Latimer hides away with the watch, which tells him to keep it closed. Meanwhile, Martha and Joan search upstairs in vain for the watch.

The aliens order the scarecrows to attack the school, but the creatures are mown down by machine guns, being operated by the pupils. As the aliens overpower the boy soldiers and enter the school, John, Joan and Martha are able to escape.

The matron takes John and Martha to an empty cottage. Latimer then arrives at the cottage and tells them that the watch told him to find the Doctor. The two women beg John to use the watch to become the Doctor once again, but he breaks down in tears. Joan then asks to be alone with John. He then puts his hand on the watch and sees a vision of what their lives could be together.

Sometime later, John enters the aliens' spaceship and offers them the Doctor's spirit in the watch. They accept but realise until it's too late and that John has already turned back into the Doctor, who has created an energy feedback on their ship, causing it to explode.

The aliens escape, but the Doctor punishes them all, including Baines who is suspended in time and spends the rest of his life as a scarecrow. Before the Doctor departs, he visits Joan for one last time. He invites her to come travelling with him, but she refuses. As the Tardis prepares to depart, the Doctor gives the now-empty watch back to Latimer. Later, on the trenches of World War One, it saves the lives of both Latimer and another pupil, Hutchinson.

Trivia and facts

'Human Nature' by Paul Cornell, and plotted with fellow writer Kate Orman, was originally published as a novel starring the Seventh Doctor in May 1995. The original novel saw the Doctor and his companion, archaeologist Bernice Summerfield take up residence at a school in Aberdeen. In the previous novel, *Sanctuary*, Berniece's lover, Guy de Carnac, had been killed, so the Doctor assumed human form, allowing the Time Lord to understand her grief. The book instantly became a fan favourite and there were plans in the late 1990s to include the story in a possible television revival of *Doctor Who*.

One draft of Cornell's 2006 script ended with the Doctor going to Joan's home to say goodbye. He then whispered his real name to her. 'That's a nice name,' she replied. The script readthrough with the cast was held on the afternoon of 23 November 2006, which was the 43rd anniversary of the very first episode of Doctor Who ('An Unearthly Child') first being broadcast on television.

Most of the school scenes were filmed at the Victorian gothic mansion of Treberfydd House in Brecon, although parts of Llandaff Cathedral in Cardiff and Tredegar House in Newport were also used. Several of the village scenes were filmed at St. Fagans National Museum of Welsh Life, which contains many historic buildings. These include the scenes outside the Cartwright's Cottage, where the Doctor throws a cricket ball to avert disaster, and the dance hall.

David Tennant was allowed to adlib the parts of the Doctor's message to Martha, which would be played too fast for the audience to hear. These included the fact that the best gig he had ever attended was a show by the Housemartins at the Scottish Exhibition and Conference Centre in Glasgow around December 1990, which he also talked about at length when he appeared on BBC Radio 4's Desert Island Discs in 2009.

'Blink'

Original UK airdate: 9 June 2007
Cast: David Tennant as The Doctor, Freema Agyeman as Martha Jones, Carey Mulligan as Sally Sparrow, Lucy Gaskell as Kathy Nightingale, Finlay Robertson as Larry Nightingale, Richard Cant as Malcolm Wainwright, Michael Obiora as Billy Shipton, Louis Mahony as Old Billy, Thomas Nelstop as Ben Wainwright, Ian Boldsworth as Banto and Ray Sawyer as the Desk Sergeant
Written by Steven Moffat
Directed by Hettie Macdonald
Music by Murray Gold
Produced by Phil Collinson

Filming dates: the main production ran from 20 November to 2 December 2006, with additional filming days on 7 November, 9 December 2006 and 9 January 2007
Running time: 43 minutes
Original UK viewing figures: 6.6 million

Review

To say 'Blink' was a massive hit from the moment it was first broadcast, would be an understatement. Even your posh mates, who would never watch Doctor Who in million years, have heard of 'Blink'. Obviously, they did not actually see it, because they only watch Scandinavian dramas with subtitles, but to quote the fictional actor Steven Toast, they've 'heard it's very good'.

After more than a decade, there is always a worry that when you return to a programme like 'Blink', that it's not as good as you remember it, or that it did not live up to the hype, which had fans begging for Steven Moffat to become the next Doctor Who showrunner.

But 'Blink' is still as brilliant today as it was all those years ago. It might have been the third season's 'cheap' story, with David Tennant and Freema Agyeman busy filming other episodes at the same time, but it is still very much *Doctor Who*, with the right combination of scares, laughs and tragedy. The absence of a reassuring presence like the Doctor making it even darker, as the viewers know anything could, and would happen to the characters confined to this story.

It's also fiendishly complicated but somehow manages to resolve all the plot points within the 43-minute running time. Who would have thought a story in a Doctor Who Annual could be so clever? The Weeping Angels also made an immediate impact and went on to become one of the revived show's most iconic villains. Like all the best ideas, the genius of the Weeping Angels lies in their simplicity. Everyone has seen a creepy stone statue. They are everywhere. Never mind running behind the sofa, 'Blink' is first-rate horror and truly the stuff of nightmares.

The story

On a wet and windy night, a young woman called Sally Sparrow breaks into a large abandoned house and starts to take pictures of the building's interior. As she walks around one room, she notices some words have been written on the wall. Slowly, she starts to peel back the wallpaper to reveal the full message. 'Beware the Weeping Angel. Oh, and duck! Really duck. Sally Sparrow, duck now!' She ducks and narrowly avoids a piece of rubble thrown at her from outside. She looks outside and all she can see is the stone statue of a weeping angel, with its hands covering its eyes.

Sally goes to her friend Kathy Nightingale's house and finds the image of the Doctor on every television screen in the house. He keeps saying 'don't blink'. The following day, Sally and Kathy return to the abandoned house. Sally notices the statue in the garden has moved closer to the house. The doorbell rings and Sally goes to answer, leaving Kathy on her own. The man at the door is looking for Sally Sparrow. He was told to bring an old letter to this address at this exact date and time for her. He says it is from Kathy Nightingale.

Sally searches for Kathy, but she has vanished. Kathy suddenly finds herself in a field and it is now 1920. Sally opens the letter and finds old pictures of Kathy and a letter, explaining the man at the door is her grandson. Sally heads to the DVD shop where Kathy's brother, Larry works. Larry tells Sally he has discovered an 'Easter egg' on seventeen random DVDs, all featuring the Doctor, who keeps making random remarks. Sally then goes to the local station and tells officers about the strange goings-on at the house, where Kathy vanished. DI Billy Shipton takes her to a garage, full of cars found at the house and a police box. Billy asks her out on a date.

After Sally leaves the garage, Billy turns to see four weeping angel statues. He wakes up in an alleyway in 1969, and the Doctor and Martha are waiting for him.

Back in the modern-day, Sally receives a call, asking her to visit the local hospital. When she arrives, she finds Billy, who is now an old man and close to death, waiting for her.

He gives her a message from the Doctor, telling her to look at the list of the 17 DVDs with the Easter eggs on. Sally realises the list is all the DVDs she owns. She calls Larry, and they both head to the abandoned house. Using a portable DVD player, they start to play the Easter egg and it appears that the Doctor is talking to Sally because he seems to know what she is going to say next. Larry starts to write down the conversation. The Doctor explains the weeping angels are alien creatures with the ultimate defence mechanism. Whenever they are seen by another creature, they freeze into stone. But if you turn away or blink, they can kill you. He ends by telling Sally that the angels are coming to get her.

They race to the basement, where they find the Tardis. Sally is able to get inside, and Larry slots one of the DVDs into the console. It starts to dematerialise, leaving Sally and Larry alone, surrounded by angels. Except the four angels are now facing each other and therefore unable to move. Sometime later, Sally and Larry are now running a bookshop together. One day, she spots the Doctor and Martha outside the shop. She warns him that one day he will get stuck in 1969 and gives them the transcript of the Easter egg conversation.

Trivia and facts

Writer Steven Moffat originally came up with the idea for Blink when he wrote a story for *Panini Book's Doctor Who Annual 2006*, which was published in August 2005. 'What I Did on My Christmas Holidays by Sally Sparrow' saw a 12-year old Sally Sparrow recount how she had spent Christmas at her aunt's cottage, where she had peeled back some wallpaper and found a message that said 'Help me, Sally Sparrow,' dated 24 December 1985.

The idea for the weeping angels themselves came from a Christmas holiday in Moffat's past, when his parents had taken him to a lonely hotel in Dorset, which was near an abandoned church, which contained statues of lamenting angels. Not all the cast were available for the script readthrough, so script editor Gary Russell read the parts of Malcolm and both young and old versions of Billy, while Moffat stood in for Tennant, who was resting his voice.

The spooky house was a dilapidated property on Field Park Road in Newport, which sadly no longer exists. Filming also took place on Charles Street in Newport, with Diverse Vinyl transformed into Banto's DVD's Store and then Sparrow & Nightingale – Antiquarian Books and Rare DVDs for the closing scenes. The graveyard scenes were filmed at St. Woolos Cemetery in Risca Road, Newport, while the scenes in Kathy's flat were recorded at a house on Llanfair Road in Pontcanna.

The closing montage of statues was filmed at a number of venues around Cardiff, including the Glamorgan Building, Alexandra Gardens and King Edward VII Avenue.

Moffat told Doctor Who Confidential that the montage aimed to do 'that thing at the end of the episode where you say that every statue is secretly a weeping angel'.

'Utopia'

Original UK airdate: 16 June 2007
Cast: David Tennant as The Doctor, Freema Agyeman as Martha Jones, John Barrowman as Captain Jack Harkness, Derek Jacobi as Professor Yana, Chipo Chung as Chantho, Rene Zagger as Padra, Neil Redman as Lieutenant Atillo, Paul Marc Davies as the Chieftan, Robert Forknall as the Guard, John Bell as Creet, Deborah Maclaren as Kristane, Abigail Canton as the Wiry Woman and John Simm as The Master
Written by Russell T. Davies
Directed by Graeme Harper
Music by Murray Gold
Produced by Phil Collinson
Filming dates: the main production ran from 30 January to 14 February 2007, with additional days on 15 January, 20 and 23 February and 1 March
Running time: 45 minutes
Original UK viewing figures: 7.8 million

Review

Although some critics complained at the time that *'Utopia'* was nothing more than an extended introduction to the series finale, it is still a fine episode in its own right and comes with one of the audacious cliff-hangers in the show's history. Having already rebooted the Daleks and the Cybermen, Russell T. Davies finally gets his hands on the Doctor's other arch-nemesis, the Master and updates the character for the new series.

Purists might have moaned about the revisions for a modern-day audience, but Davies handles the re-introduction of the Master beautifully, with some clever audio samples from the original series for good measure. Special mention must go to Derek Jacobi for his performance, both first as the brave

Professor Yana and then as the Master himself. Better critics than me have hailed him as one of the greatest actors of our generation, but to see the newly restored Master turn around and face the camera directly is truly spine-chilling stuff. It seems a pity to have him regenerate so quickly into the John Simm incarnation, but Professor Yana's demise serves a much greater purpose – namely the plot itself. At least Big Finish were able to bring Jacobi back for some more masterful action on audio.

Director Graeme Harper ensures that the action keeps moving and even if humanity's search for a new world feels like it has been tagged on at times, Utopia is all about the central characters. By the end of the story, the Doctor's world has changed irrevocably, with the Face of Boe's prophecy from 'Gridlock' coming back to haunt him. The Doctor is no longer alone and is left trapped at the end of time. The stakes really do not get higher than this!

The story

The Doctor has parked the Tardis above a time rift in Cardiff Bay, hoping to refuel his time machine. But his arrival has come to the attention of an old friend, Captain Jack Harkness, who races across the Bay, eager to see him again. As Jack gets near, the Tardis starts to dematerialise. Jack hurls himself at the time machine and clings on to the outside, as it flies through the time vortex.

The Tardis lands on a dark, desolate planet, somewhere near the end of the universe. The Doctor and Martha step out of the Tardis and find Jack lying on the ground, seemingly dead. But he soon comes back to life and starts flirting with Martha.

As they explore, the three of them find a man being hunted by a savage group of humanoid creatures, known as the Futurekind. They are chased towards a gated missile silo, where they find the last remaining humans on the planet.

Inside, the Doctor, Jack and Martha meet a kindly, old man called Professor Yana and his insectoid assistant, Chantho. The Professor explains they have built a rocket to take them all to a planet called Utopia, but the engine is not working. The Doctor offers to help.

As the Doctor and the Professor work together to fix the rocket, the Professor admits he hears a constant drumming noise in his head. Some of the people in the silo head out into the wasteland and bring the Tardis back to the Professor's laboratory. The sight of the police box appears to have a strange effect on the Professor. The Doctor uses his time machine to provide extra power for the rocket and it is now fully operational. As the survivors start to board, one of the Futurekind, who has sneaked onto the base, smashes the power controls, causing the chamber to be flooded with radiation.

As Jack cannot die, he heads into the chamber to fix the problem. While in the chamber, he talks to the Doctor, who is on the other side of the chamber door. Professor Yana is also listening in via the intercom, and the conversation starts to trigger something else in his mind.

Right: 'So, where was I? Oh, that's right! Barcelona!' The Tenth Doctor makes his very first appearance at the end of the Season One finale 'The Parting of the Ways'. (*BBC*)

Left: The Tenth Doctor comes face to face with the legendary Madame de Pompadour (Sophia Myles) in the Season Two story 'The Girl in the Fireplace'. (*BBC*)

Right: The Cybermen get a major upgrade and return to Doctor Who in the Season Two two-parter 'Rise of the Cybermen/The Age of Steel'. (*BBC*)

Left: The Torchwood Institute plays a key role during Season Two and in the finale, 'Army of Ghosts/ Doomsday', it is revealed that Yvonne Hartman (Tracy-Ann Oberman) is now the director of Torchwood London. (*BBC*)

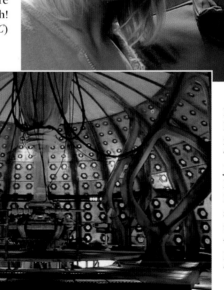

Right: Under Hartman's instructions, Torchwood London opens an interdimensional breach, which heralds the return of both the Cybermen and the Daleks, but Rose Tyler (Billie Piper) and Mickey Smith (Noel Clarke) are ready to defend the Earth! (*BBC*)

Left: Despite having many friends, like Rose Tyler, Martha Jones and Donna Noble, the Tenth Doctor could cut a lonely figure at times, particularly when he was on his own in the Tardis. (*BBC*)

Right: Just seconds after he says a tearful goodbye to Rose, the Doctor realises in 'The Runaway Bride' that he is not alone in the Tardis. Her name is Donna Noble (Catherine Tate) and she is not best pleased. (*BBC*)

Left: Have you met Miss Jones? Season Three sees the introduction of a new companion in the shape of the ever-resourceful Martha Jones (Freema Agyeman), who makes her first appearance in 'Smith and Jones'. (*BBC*)

Right: Bard to the bone! The Doctor and Martha Jones meet none other than the legendary playwright William Shakespeare (Dean Lennox Kelly) in 'The Shakespeare Code', which was partly filmed at the Globe Theatre in London. (*BBC*)

Left: Trying to flee a group of aliens eager to steal his life force, the Doctor takes on the new identity of teacher John Smith in 1913, in the Season Three two-part adventure 'Human Nature/The Family of Blood'. But while he works at the school, Smith meets school nurse Joan Redfern (Jessica Hynes) and they fall in love. (*BBC*)

Right: Sally Sparrow (Carey Mulligan) investigates the strange goings on at the abandoned house Wester Drumlins in the multi-award-winning Season Three story 'Blink'. (*BBC*)

Left: The mysterious Harold Saxon turns out to be none other than Doctor's arch nemesis and fellow Time Lord, the Master (John Simm) in the Season Three finale 'The Sound of Drums/Last of the Time Lords'. (*BBC*)

Right: After defeating the Master, Captain Jack Harkness (John Barrowman), the Doctor and Martha Jones say their goodbyes in 'Last of the Time Lords'. But Captain Jack has one final revelation. He used to be known as the Face of Boe. (*BBC*)

Left: She should be so lucky. Waitress Astrid Peth (Kylie Minogue) meets the Doctor, while onboard the interstellar line Titanic in the 2007 Christmas special 'Voyage of the Damned'. (*BBC*)

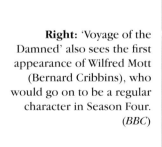

Right: 'Voyage of the Damned' also sees the first appearance of Wilfred Mott (Bernard Cribbins), who would go on to be a regular character in Season Four. (*BBC*)

Left: Season Four also saw the return of Donna Noble (Catherine Tate), who travelled with the Doctor on many adventures, including back in time to witness the eruption of Mount Vesuvius in 'The Fires of Pompeii'. (*BBC*)

Right: The Doctor and Donna meet the servant alien creatures the Ood in the Season Four story, 'Planet of the Ood'. (*BBC*)

Left: 'Hello Dad!' In 'The Doctor's Daughter', the Time Lord has a tissue sample extracted from his hand, which in turn is used to create Jenny (Georgia Moffett). (*BBC*)

Right: Spoilers! The Season Four tale 'Silence in the Library' saw the debut of Professor River Song (Alex Kingston), who would go on to play a big role in future adventures starring the Eleventh (Matt Smith) and Twelfth Doctor (Peter Capaldi). (*BBC*)

Left: When worlds collide. In 'Turn Left', Rose Tyler and Donna Noble join forces in a world where the Doctor no longer exists. (*BBC*)

Right: The final run of specials kicked off in December 2008 with 'The Next Doctor', which teamed the Time Lord up with Jackson Lake (David Morrissey) on Christmas Eve, 1851. (*BBC*)

Left: The Tenth Doctor's darkest hour came in 'The Waters of Mars', when he tried to help Captain Adelaide Brooke (Lindsay Duncan) and the crew of the Martian colony Bowie Base One. (*BBC*)

Right: 'I don't want to go...' After sending the Master and the rest of the Time Lords back into the Time War, and saving Wilfred Mott, the Tenth Doctor says his final words before regenerating in 'The End of Time'. (*BBC*)

Left: But it was far from being all over as the Tenth Doctor returned in the 50th anniversary special 'The Day of the Doctor', alongside Matt Smith as the Eleventh Doctor and the War Doctor (John Hurt). (*BBC*)

Right: The Brandon Estate in South London. The Southwark council estate doubles as the Powell Estate, where Rose Tyler lived and appears in 'The Christmas Invasion' and 'The End of Time'. (*Jamie Hailstone*)

Left: Clearwell Caves in the Forest of Dean, Gloucestershire. The caves were used to film scenes onboard the Sycorax spaceship in 'The Christmas Invasion', as well as scenes in 'The Satan Pit'. (*Jamie Hailstone*)

Right: Wales Millennium Centre, Cardiff Bay. The outside of the Millennium Centre features in 'Utopia', while the inside foyer was used to film some of the hospital scenes in 'New Earth'. (*Jamie Hailstone*)

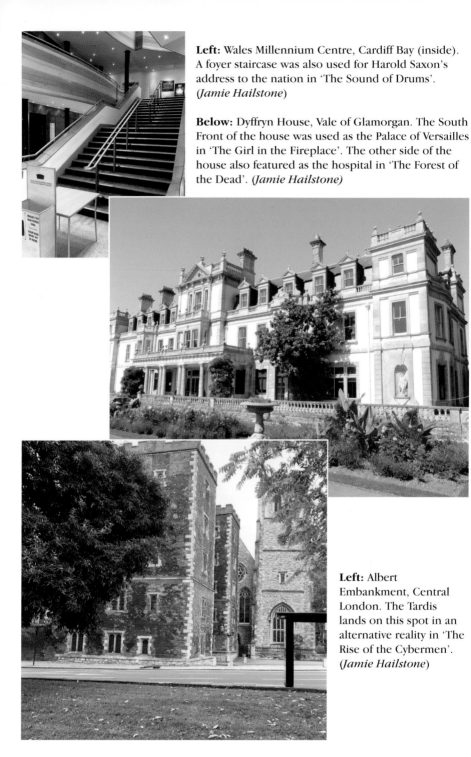

Left: Wales Millennium Centre, Cardiff Bay (inside). A foyer staircase was also used for Harold Saxon's address to the nation in 'The Sound of Drums'. (*Jamie Hailstone*)

Below: Dyffryn House, Vale of Glamorgan. The South Front of the house was used as the Palace of Versailles in 'The Girl in the Fireplace'. The other side of the house also featured as the hospital in 'The Forest of the Dead'. (*Jamie Hailstone*)

Left: Albert Embankment, Central London. The Tardis lands on this spot in an alternative reality in 'The Rise of the Cybermen'. (*Jamie Hailstone*)

Right: Southerndown Beach (also known as Dunraven Bay), Glamorgan. The beach is better known as Bad Wolf Bay and features in 'Doomsday' and 'Journey's End'. (*Jamie Hailstone*)

Left: Atradius, Cardiff Bay. The building used to film scenes at the offices of H.C. Clements during 'The Runaway Bride'. (*Jamie Hailstone*)

Below: The Globe Theatre, Central London. Doctor Who became the first drama to ever film at the venue for 'The Shakespeare Code'. (*Jamie Hailstone*)

Left: Bute Park, Cardiff. The central Cardiff park was transformed into New York's famous Central Park for 'Daleks in Manhattan' and 'Evolution of the Daleks'. (*Jamie Hailstone*)

Right: The Senedd (National Assembly for Wales), Cardiff Bay. The foyer of the Senedd was used to film the party scenes in 'The Lazarus Experiment'. (*Jamie Hailstone*)

Left: Wells Cathedral, Somerset. The gothic cathedral doubled for Southwark Cathedral during the final scenes of 'The Lazarus Experiment'. (*Jamie Hailstone*)

Right: Oakdale Workmen's Institute, St. Fagans National Museum of History, Cardiff. The building, which dates back to 1917, was used as the village hall in 'Human Nature' and 'The Family of Blood'. (*Jamie Hailstone*)

Left: Gwalia Stores, St. Fagans National Museum of History, Cardiff. The shop front also appears in 'Human Nature', when John Smith throws a cricket ball to save a baby being crushed by a piano. (*Jamie Hailstone*)

Right: Melin Bompren Corn Mill, St. Fagans National Museum of History, Cardiff. The Mill became the Cartwright's abandoned cottage in 'The Family of Blood'. (*Jamie Hailstone*)

Left: Diverse Vinyl, Newport. The independent record store was transformed into Banto's DVD Store and then into Sparrow & Nightingale for 'Blink'. (*Jamie Hailstone*)

Right: Castell Coch, Cardiff. The castle was the German UNIT base, where Martha Jones flees from the Daleks in 'Journey's End'. (*Jamie Hailstone*)

Left: Millers Green, Gloucester. The small square on the grounds of Gloucester Cathedral, was used to film the Victorian Christmas fair in 'The Next Doctor'. (*Jamie Hailstone*)

Right: The entrance to Millers Green, Gloucester. The square is linked to the main cathedral grounds by a small passageway, which is where the Tardis materialised in 'The Next Doctor'. *(Jamie Hailstone)*

Left: The National Museum of Wales, Cardiff. Lady Christina's daring heist at the beginning of 'Planet of the Dead' was filmed in the museum lobby. *(Jamie Hailstone)*

Right: Victoria Place, Newport. The road was used for climatic final scenes of 'The Waters of Mars', when the Tardis comes back to Earth and the Tenth Doctor faces the consequences of his actions. *(Jamie Hailstone)*

Left: Caerphilly Castle, Caerphilly. The castle has become a popular venue for Doctor Who over the years, but in the case of the Tenth Doctor it appears only once. (*Jamie Hailstone*)

Right: Caerphilly Castle's gatehouse doubles for the prison in which Lucy Saxon is held captive and the Master is brought back to life in 'The End of Time'. (*Jamie Hailstone*)

Left: St. Mary's Church, Marshfield, Newport. The church was used to film Donna Noble's wedding and the Tenth Doctor's final goodbyes to Wilfred Mott and Sylvia Noble in 'The End of Time'. (*Jamie Hailstone*)

Martha notices the Professor also carries a fob watch, which is similar to the one the Doctor used to become human in 'Human Nature/Family of Blood'. She runs down to the chamber room and tells the Doctor that he might be alone after all. As the rocket blasts off, the drumming noises inside the Professor's head get even louder and he opens the watch. Suddenly, the Doctor remembers the Face of Boe's final words 'You are not alone' or Y-A-N-A for short.

Inside the laboratory, Professor Yana is no more. He is the Doctor's arch-enemy, the Master. He shoots Chantho and enters the Tardis, just as the Doctor, Jack and Martha race back to the laboratory. The Master locks the Tardis door and regenerates. The renegade Time Lord then dematerialises, leaving the Doctor, Jack and Martha stranded at the end of the universe and at the mercy of the Futurekind.

Trivia and facts

Following on from the previous year's *Blue Peter* competition to design a monster (which appeared in 'Love & Monsters'), the long-running children's programme went one further and announced on Monday, 16 October 2006 they would be giving viewers under the age of 14 the chance to win a part in an upcoming episode, which turned out to be 'Utopia'. After a gruelling selection process, nine-year-old John Bell was chosen to play the character of Creed in the story.

Sir Derek Jacobi had already played the Master in the 2003 BBC online animated serial 'Scream of the Shalka', which was written by Paul Cornell. The readthrough was held on the same day as the readthrough for '42' with script editor Gary Russell reading David Tennant's lines, who was still recuperating.

To mark the return of John Barrowman to the Doctor Who set, the cast put a sign that read 'Doctor Poo' on his trailer, while Tennant's was christened 'Captain Jock'.

To prevent his identity leaking out, John Simm was billed as 'The Enemy' on call sheets for the episode. As the Professor's fob watch opens, the voices of previous versions of the Master can be heard, including Roger Delgado shouting at Azal from the 1971 story 'The Daemons'. The old NEG Glass Site in Trident Park, Cardiff and Wenvoe Quarry were used for the external scenes, while the scenes of Captain Jack running towards the Tardis were filmed outside the Millennium Centre in Cardiff Bay.

'The Sound of Drums/Last of the Time Lords'

Original UK airdate: 23/30 June 2007
Cast: David Tennant as The Doctor, Freema Agyeman as Martha Jones, John Barrowman as Captain Jack Harkness, John Simm as The Master, Adjoa Andoh as Francine Jones, Gugu Mbatha-Raw as Tish Jones, Trevor Laird as Clive Jones, Reggie Yates as Leo Jones, Alexandra Moen as Lucy Saxon, Colin Stinton as the President, Nichola McAuliffe as Vivien Rook, Nicholas Gecks as Albert Dumfries, Sharon Osbourne as Herself, McFly as Themselves, Ann Widdecombe as Herself,

Olivia Hill as BBC Newsreader, Lachele Carl as US Newsreader, Daniel Ming as Chinese Newsreader, Elize Du Toit as the Sinister Woman, Zoe Thorne, Gerard Logan and Johnnie Lyne-Pirkis as Sphere Voices, Tom Ellis as Thomas Milligan, Ellie Haddington as Professor Docherty, Tom Golding as the Lad and Natasha Alexander
Written by Russell T. Davies
Directed by Colin Teague
Music by Murray Gold
Produced by Phil Collinson
Filming dates: the main production ran from 7 February to 19 March 2007
Running time: 46/51 minutes
Original UK viewing figures: 7.5/8.6 million

Review

There is a lot to say about the third series finale. There is no denying that it is an epic finish to a highly satisfying series, but it is not without its flaws. A large sticking point has to be John Simm's portrayal of the Master. While pairing Tennant against a younger, sexier Master makes perfect sense, this version of the evil Time Lord seems to be sandwiched somewhere between Jack Nicholson's Joker and the manic energy of Frank Gorshin's Riddler. Later appearances by Simm as the Master were toned down and were all the better for it, but in 'The Sound of Drums/Last of the Time Lords', he was pretty annoying.

The second point has to be one of the rare CGI fails in modern-day Doctor Who, which is the heavily aged Doctor in the second half of the story. With the best will in the world, he looks like the poor relative of Dobby the House Elf from the Harry Potter franchise. And then there is a resolution of the story itself, in which the entire population of Earth stand together and think of the Doctor, despite the fact that most of them have never met him. If you have not reached for the sick bag by that point, you then have to endure the sight of the Doctor floating through the air and giving the Master a big hug. The sentiment is noble, but the delivery feels like He-Man facing the camera at the end of the 1980s cartoon and reminding us all to eat our vegetables and always remember to look before we cross the road.

If there is a redeeming feature of this finale, it is the resolution of the Martha Jones plot. Seeing her part with the Doctor on her own terms, having recognised that parts of their relationship are unhealthy, is deeply satisfying and a timely reminder that Russell T. Davies can do proper drama, as well as overblown space opera.

Of course, the subtlety does not last too long and once again, the series ends on an eyebrow-raising cliffhanger. Next stop, the Titanic and a certain Australian pop princess...

The story

Using Jack's vortex manipulator, the Doctor, Jack and Martha escape from the silo and land back on modern-day Earth. Martha says he recognised the voice of the newly regenerated Master and that he sounded just like a politician called Harold Saxon. As they walk down the street, large television screens on the streets announce the results of the general election and Harold Saxon – aka the Master - is the new prime minister.

Inside Downing Street, Martha's sister, Tish Jones has been hired. When she asks Saxon what she should do, he tells her to 'stand there and look gorgeous'. In another part of Downing Street, journalist Vivien Rook says she is here to interview Lucy Saxon, the new prime minister's wife. When they are alone, Vivien warns Lucy that she is in great danger and everything about Harold Saxon is a lie.

Saxon enters the room and admits he is the Master. He then introduces Vivien to his friends, spheres with spinning blades known as the Toclafane, who murder the journalist.

Back in Martha's flat, the Doctor, Jack and Martha watch a television broadcast in which the prime minister has been contacted by a new alien species – the Toclafane – who will appear on Earth the following day. The Doctor turns the television around and discovers a bomb. They all run out of the flat, and it explodes. Worried, Martha immediately calls her mother but when Francine mentions she has got back together with her ex-husband, Clive, Martha realises it is a trap.

Martha drives to her mother's house and sees her family being bundled into a van. Armed police officers open fire and they drive off. The Doctor realises the Master has used the Archangel Network (first mentioned in 'The Christmas Invasion') to hypnotise the world. The following day, the Master and the President of the United States head to the flying aircraft carrier Valiant for first contact with the Toclafane. The Doctor, Jack and Martha also smuggle themselves on the carrier. Onboard, the Doctor discovers the Master has turned his Tardis into a paradox machine. They head to the bridge, where the Master uses his laser screwdriver to blast Jack and guards grab the Doctor. The Master then uses technology developed by Professor Lazarus ('The Lazarus Experiment') to age the Doctor by 100 years. The sky above the Valiant rip open and billions of Toclafane head down to the Earth below. The Doctor whispers something to Martha, who uses Jack's vortex manipulator to escape and return to Earth.

One year later, Martha arrives on an empty beach and meets a young man, called Tom Milligan, who shows her to a fleet of rockets. Up on the Valiant, the Master has enslaved Martha's family, imprisoned Jack and keeps taunting the aged Doctor. He then uses his laser screwdriver to suspend the Doctor's ability to regenerate, causing him to age a full 900 years. Tom is able to stun a Toclafane with an electrical charge. Another member of the resistance, Professor Dochertyopens up the Toclafane and finds a human head inside. It recognises Martha from the missile silo at the end of the universe ('Utopia').

Martha realises the Toclafane are the human race from the future and that's why the Master needs a paradox machine because the Toclafane cannot murder their own ancestors. Martha has heard of a weapon developed by UNIT and Torchwood, which is capable of killing a Time Lord by injecting them with four chemicals. Martha has three of the chemicals. The last one is on a UNIT base in North London. Tom offers to take Martha there, but they are both betrayed by Professor Docherty, who reports them to the Master.

The Master captures Martha and takes her back on board the Valiant, where she tells him the story about the gun was a lie. She has actually been travelling all over the world, telling them at an allotted time to think of one word –'Doctor'.

When every human being starts to think of the Doctor it creates a telepathic field, which restores the Doctor to his former self. Jack fights his way into the Tardis and destroys the paradox machine. With the machine destroyed, time reverses by a year and a day. Lucy Saxon shoots the Master, who refuses to regenerate and dies in the Doctor's arms. Back on Earth, Jack says goodbye to the Doctor and Martha. As he leaves, he jokes that he might live for a million years and that his nickname as a child was the Face of Boe. In the Tardis, the Doctor offers to take Martha on another adventure, but she refuses. Instead, she leaves to care for her family. After Martha leaves, the Doctor is stunned when the bow of a ship called the Titanic bursts through the walls of the Tardis.

Trivia and facts

Russell T. Davies originally came up with the idea of the Toclafane in 2004, when the production team thought they had lost the rights to use the Daleks during production of the first series and had to come up with an alternative for Robert Shearman's 'Dalek's script.'They weren't called Toclafane back then, they were just Future Humans,' explained Davies in the 2010 book *Doctor Who: The Writer's Tale – The Final Chapter*.

A big inspiration for Davies was the 2005 track Voodoo Child by Rogue Traders, which includes the lyrics 'Here it comes/The sound of drums'. Davies asked script editor Simon Winstone to clear the song's use very early in the production for series three, as the clearance process can be quite time-consuming. But as work continued on the script, the showrunner forgot about the song and had to be reminded by Winstone that it had been cleared and paid for several months later. Some script changes had to be made to keep costs down. For example, Davies had envisaged a bigger car chase in 'The Sound of Drums', where Martha drove through gardens with the police in hot pursuit.

Reggie Yates, who played Leo Jones earlier in the series, was busy on various projects for Radio 1 and could only be spared for one day's filming, which meant his character's involvement was also scaled back. The first filming for the two episodes was on 7 February 2007 at Upper Boat Studios. There was then a small break before recording started in earnest at Hensol Castle on 15 February, where some of the Downing Street scenes were filmed. The Master's election victory speech was recorded on a stairway inside the Millennium Centre in Cardiff Bay, while the area of Roundwood and the Maelfa Shopping Centre in Llanedeyrn acted as the precinct where the Doctor, Martha and

Captain Jack abandoned the car. The scenes on board the flight deck of the Valiant were recorded at Upper Boat Studios. The lower deck scenes were filmed at the old NEG Glass site in Trident Park, which also featured heavily in previous episodes, like '42'.

The hand of production manager Tracie Simpson picked up the Master's ring after the funeral pyre when his body is cremated. David Tennant and John Barrowman's last day on set for the third series was a night shoot, which started at 5 pm on 10 March 2007 and finished at 4 am the following morning (11 March). During filming Barrowman turned 40 at midnight and cast and crew celebrated with a Dalek birthday cake and champagne.

Filming then continued until 16 March 2007, with just Freema Agyeman from the main cast.

Season Four

'Voyage of the Damned'
Original UK airdate: 25 December 2007
Cast: David Tennant as The Doctor, Kylie Minogue as Astrid Peth, Geoffrey Palmer as Captain Hardaker, Russell Tovey as Midshipman Frame, George Costigan as Max Capricorn, Gary O'Brien as Rickston Slade, Andrew Havill as Chief Steward, Bruce Lawrence as the Engineer, Debbie Chazen as Foon Van Hoff, Clive Rowe as Marvin Van Hoff, Clive Swift as Mr Copper, Jimmy Vee as Bannakaffalatta, Bernard Cribbins as Wilfred Mott, Nicholas Witchell as Himself, Paul Kasey as The Host, Stefan Davis as the Kitchen Hand, Jason Mohammad as the Newsreader, Colin McFarlane and Ewan Bailey as alien voices and Jessica Martin as the Queen
Written by Russell T. Davies
Directed by James Strong
Music by Murray Gold
Produced by Phil Collinson
Filming dates: the main filming block ran from 9 July to 8 August 2007, with additional filming days on 21 August and 20 October
Running time: 71 minutes
Original UK viewing figures: 13.3 million

Review
Having come to the conclusion that viewers on a Christmas Day want nothing more than a bit of fun, Russell T. Davies serves up a terrific homage to the great disaster movies of the 1970s. Disaster movies were always a guilty pleasure, even in their heyday. The opening of every skyscraper always ends in a massive explosion, every flight across America contains at least one washed-up quarterback and a group of nuns and there's always a hero who says 'to hell with the rules' and gets the love interest out alive, even if everyone else snuffs it in the process.

'Voyage of the Damned' is the guiltiest of pleasures, revelling in all the clichés of the genre. There's a washed-up ship captain, a rookie midshipman, who is out on his first voyage, and a gang of survivors, who you just know will get picked off, one-by-one. The stunt casting of Kylie Minogue ensured that the special was on the front page of every television listings magazine published at the time, and while there was a certain element of 'something for the dad's', the Australian pop princess proves she is a fine actress, displaying terrific chemistry with David Tennant. If only she could have been persuaded to put that singing lark on hold, she might have made something of herself. She might even have had her own Big Finish spin-off series by now.

'Voyage of the Damned' also gives Tennant the chance to play the Tenth Doctor at his most heroic. When he faces the camera and says he is going to save everyone, you believe it. The sight of the Doctor being carried by the angelic host robots might be a bit over the top, but 'Voyage of the Damned' is best viewed as a festive rollercoaster. Watched at any other time of the year, it's total nonsense. Just buckle up and pass the mince pies.

The story

An old-fashioned sea liner, bearing the name Titanic crashes through the walls of the Tardis. The Doctor acts quickly to repair the danger and then materialises on board. To his astonishment, he finds it is a large spaceship orbiting above the Earth and has been built to look exactly like the ill-fated ship, which sank on its maiden voyage in 1912. Up on the ship's bridge, the long-serving Captain Hardaker dismisses his officers for a tot of rum. But one young officer, Midshipman Frame elects to stay, citing regulations that the bridge must be staffed by two officers at all times.

Downstairs, a lavish Christmas party is in full swing. As he walks around, the Doctor befriends a beautiful waitress called Astrid Peth, and two passengers, Morvin and Foon Van Hoff, who won their tickets to be onboard, in a competition. The Doctor decides to join the Van Hoffs on a 'shore leave' trip down to the Earth and drags Astrid along for the ride. They are accompanied by the ship's historian, Mr Cooper, who has some very strange ideas about the local culture. He tells them that the UK is ruled by Good King Wenceslas and every Christmas Eve, Britain goes to war with Turkey.

The tour group teleport down to the surface, but the streets of London are deserted. They return to the ship and the Doctor spots a meteor shower heading towards the Titanic. He tries to raise the alarm but is taken away by the Chief Steward. On the bridge, Midshipman Frame also sees the meteors. He tries to put the shields back up but is stopped by Captain Hardaker, who shoots him. The meteors strike the ship, causing explosions throughout the vessel. As the Titanic starts to drift through space, the Doctor gathers a small group of survivors, including Astrid, and promises to take them to safety.

The Doctor contacts the bridge and finds that Midshipman Frame is still alive. The Doctor and his group climb through the wreckage, towards the bridge, but they find the ship's angelic host robots have a new mission – to kill any survivors.

The Host robots capture the Doctor and take him to Deck 31, where he meets the Titanic's owner, Max Capricorn in a life support unit. His cruise liner business has failed, and he wants to crash the ship into the Earth and frame his fellow board members with murder. Max deactivates the ship's engines. Astrid appears and drives a forklift truck into the support unit containing Max and pushes them both into the ship's engines. Two Host robots carry the Doctor up to the bridge as the Titanic plummets into the Earth's atmosphere. At the last moment, the Doctor is able to pull the Titanic out of its steep dive, narrowly avoiding Buckingham Palace and returns the vessel to orbit.

Trivia and facts

The casting of Kylie Minogue came about after the pop princess's creative director, Will Baker, attended the press launch of *Doctor Who's* 2007 series at the Mayfair Hotel in London. Baker got chatting to the programme's senior brand manager, Edward Russell at the event, who in turn introduced him to Julie Gardner and casting director Andy Pryor. Both Gardner and Pryor mentioned that if Minogue ever found the time, they would love to have her on the show as a guest star. The following day, Baker contacted Russell and asked for a copy of 'The Runaway Bride', so he could show it to her. A few days later (26 March 2007), Baker called Russell to say she might be interested.

'Voyage of the Damned' almost had another guest star in the shape of Hollywood legend, Dennis Hopper. Director James Strong met Hopper's agent on a flight back to the UK, who was interested in appearing in the show. The part of Mr Copper was offered to the star, but it later transpired that the star of Easy Rider and Speed would only be available for four days filming, so the idea was dropped. Russell T. Davies' original description of the Christmas special was 'The Titanic in Space crossed with the Poseidon Adventure'.

The script readthrough occurred at the Central Baptist Church on Shaftesbury Avenue on 2 July 2007, although it was slightly delayed after a photographer from The Sun was discovered hiding in a cupboard and then asked to leave. Production on 'Voyage of the Damned' started at Upper Boat studios on9 July 2007. To keep the casting of Kylie Minogue a secret, the call sheets simply said that Astrid would be played by 'Astrid'.

The empty Exchange Building on Adelaide Street in Swansea was used to film some of the reception scenes and had been previously glimpsed in the first series story 'The Unquiet Dead'. While filming took place, BBC News carried a story that Minogue had been mistaken for a real waitress outside a hotel in Swansea, when an elderly customer thought she was a member of staff. The Queen's voice was provided by actress Jessica Martin, who had played Mags in the 1988/89 Doctor Who story 'The Greatest Show in the Galaxy'.

Bernard Cribbins' character was originally called Stan in the script and intended as a one-off appearance. However, as work started on the fourth series, it became clear that Howard Attfield – who had played Geoff Noble in 'The Runaway Bride'– was seriously ill. Attfield completed a few scenes for 'Partners in Crime', but when it was apparent that he would not be able to continue, Phil Collinson suggested rewriting the part and casting Cribbins as Donna's grandfather. Davies then took the opportunity to rename Cribbins character in 'Voyage of the Damned' as Wilfred 'Wilf' Mott.

'Partners in Crime'

Original UK airdate: 5 April 2008
Cast: David Tennant as The Doctor, Catherine Tate as Donna Noble, Billie Piper as Rose Tyler, Sarah Lancashire as Miss Foster, Bernard Cribbins as Wilfred Mott, Jacqueline King as Sylvia Noble, Verona Joseph as Penny Carter, Jessica Gunning

as Stacey Campbell, Martin Ball as Roger Davey, Rachid Sabitri as Craig Staniland, Chandra Ruegg as Clare Pope, Sue Kelvin as Suzette Chambers and Jonathan Stratt as the Taxi Driver
Written by Russell T. Davis
Directed by James Strong
Music by Murray Gold
Produced by Phil Collinson
Filming dates: the main production ran from 4 October to 20 November 2007, with additional filming days on 27 and 29 November, and 18 December
Running time: 48 minutes
Original UK viewing figures: 9.1 million

Review

By the time *Doctor Who* returned to British screens in 2008 with the Tenth Doctor's third series, there was always a danger that the viewing public would start to tire of the Time Lord. And having already given us a love story in the shape of the Doctor and Rose Tyler, a warning on the dangers of unrequited love with Martha Jones, and Kylie Minogue in a maid's outfit, it was clearly time to try something new.

For the Tenth Doctor's final series, the Time Lord's companion would be nothing more than a good old-fashioned mate to have some fun with. 'Partners in Crime' sets up the template for the series, with plenty of slapstick. It's a romp, making the most of both David Tennant and Catherine Tate's finely tuned comic sensibilities. It also wisely keeps the two main characters apart for as long as humanly possible, with some brilliant direction from James Strong.

You can practically hear Russell T. Davies sniggering away as he types in all the dialogue about slimming pills. The fat just walks away indeed. The fourth series would feature some of his darkest writing, particularly on 'Midnight' and 'Turn Left', but 'Partners in Crime' is frothier than a gas station cappuccino. Sarah Lancashire appears to be enjoying herself a little too much as Miss Foster and it really is a shame that the character meets at an untimely end at the programme's conclusion, because she would have made a great recurring villain.

As for the Adipose aliens themselves, you will either find them endearing and cute, or very annoying. For me, they fall into the incredibly annoying category. It is one of those few times when you start to wonder if the monster has been specifically designed so it can be sold at conventions as a toy. It's all about the merchandise these days.

The story

The Doctor is investigating the strange goings-on at Adipose Industries, unaware that his old friend Donna Noble ('The Runaway Bride') is also on the case. They both attend a presentation by the stern-looking Adipose boss Miss Foster, which has developed a 100% legal pill that helps people lose weight.

'The fat just walks away,' says Miss Foster. The capsules are already available in London and they plan to roll them out across the rest of the country. The Doctor and Donna both get lists of Adipose customers and head off, separately to find out more.

Donna meets a customer called Stacey Campbell, who has lost eleven pounds in the five days since she started taking the pills. Stacey nips up to the bathroom. Suddenly a small, blobby creature detaches itself from her stomach. Then she dissolves into even more of the creatures, who start to escape through the bathroom window. Hearing her screams, Donna races upstairs and sees the last creature jump through the window.

The Doctor and Donna then separately return to the offices of Adipose Industries. Donna hides in the toilets when Miss Foster and her guards enter. They kick open the cubicles, but before they can find Donna, they find a journalist called Penny Carter and take her up to Miss Foster's office.

Up in the office, Miss Foster explains the pills turn fat into small alien creatures called Adipose. Donna looks in through the office door window, and the Doctor watches from outside, standing in a window cleaner's cradle. Suddenly, the two of them spot each other. Then Miss Foster sees them both and they have to run.

The Doctor and Donna are finally reunited, but also run into Miss Foster and her guards. She tells them she has been hired to foster a new generation of Adipose after their homeworld was lost.

A spaceship appears in the sky, and all the Adipose creatures head to the streets, where they are teleported up into the ship. The Doctor warns Miss Foster that the Adipose intend to kill her, but she ignores him. The Adipose spaceship zooms away and she falls to her death.

Donna accepts the Doctor's offer to go travelling in the Tardis. Donna's parked her mum's car near the Tardis. She phones her mum and tells her that the car keys are in a bin nearby. She then tells one of the bystanders to look out for her mum, but that bystander is none other than Rose Tyler. As the crowds thin, Rose Tyler walks away and vanishes into thin air.

Trivia and facts

When Russell T. Davies started to draw up plans for the fourth series of *Doctor Who*, he came up with the character of Penny Carter, who would be around 30, jilted and be blunt about some things and gobsmacked by others. When Davies discussed his plans with executive producer Julie Gardner and BBC head of fiction Jane Tranter, it was suggested that they really needed someone like Donna Noble, who had appeared as a one-off character in 'The Runaway Bride'. A few days later, Tranter informed the production team that she would be willing to return for an entire season.

As previously mentioned, Howard Attfield was also due to return as Donna's father and completed the filming of several scenes for 'Partners in Crime', before pulling out due to ill-health. The scenes are included in the Series 4

DVD boxset. Attfield died on 31 October 2007 and he was given a special credit at the end of 'Partners in Crime', which read 'In Memory of Howard Attfield 1947-2007'.

The boss of Adipose Industries was originally called Miss Rattigan and described in the script as '40s, handsome, strong, very Amanda Redman'. The character's name was later changed to Miss Foster because Rattigan reminded Davies of the Walt Disney film The Great Mouse Detective. The end of the script included a brief scene in which Donna spoke to a woman, who turned out to be Rose Tyler. To keep this a secret, the scene was marked 'Omitted' in the shooting scripts and recorded in a later filming block.

'The Fires of Pompeii'

Original UK airdate: 12 April 2008
Cast: David Tennant as The Doctor, Catherine Tate as Donna Noble, Phil Cornwell as the Stallholder, Karen Gillan as the Soothsayer, Sasha Behar as Spurrina, Lorraine Burroughs as Thalina, Peter Capaldi as Caecilius, Tracey Childs as Metella, Francesca Fowler as Evelina, Francois Pandolfo as Quintus, Victoria Wicks as the High Priestess, Gerard Bell as Major Domo and Phil Davis as Lucius
Written by James Moran
Directed by Colin Teague
Music by Murray Gold
Produced by Phil Collinson
Filming dates: the main production ran from 13 September to 2 October 2007, with an additional filming day on 20 October
Running time: 48 minutes
Original UK viewing figures: 9 million

Review

Back in the good old days, nobody ever dared question why the Doctor did not hop in the Tardis and prevent something really bad from happening in the first place. After all, what's the point of having a time machine, if you can't alter history?

With the revived series and a more questioning audience, the scripts started to emphasise that certain events were 'fixed points in time' and could not be changed.

In stark contrast to the comedic 'Partners in Crime', 'The Fires of Pompeii' gets serious by addressing the moral implications of the Doctor's knowledge and what he can and cannot do. It also gives the show a new lease of life by having the companion properly challenge the Time Lord over his decisions. There are a couple of decent gags about what happens when the Doctor and the companion try to quote Latin sayings at the Romans. Thanks to the Tardis translation circuits, the natives think they are speaking Welsh. Who knew?

The production team were also able to make the most of filming abroad by utilising the Cinecitta Studios in Rome. The Doctor Who team might only have been there for a few days, but there's no doubt it gives the episode a strong visual look.

The only drawback is the Pyrovile aliens themselves. They might tick all the right volcanic boxes, but they are instantly forgettable. 'The Fires of Pompeii' is also noticeable for featuring Karen Gillan (Amy Pond) and Peter Capaldi (the Twelfth Doctor), although both are playing very different roles. Capaldi, in particular, is far more subtle and restrained than he ever was when he became the Doctor, proving he is one of the most versatile actors to have ever played the Time Lord.

The story

The Doctor takes Donna to Ancient Rome, or at least he thinks he has. Instead, they have arrived in Pompeii and it's the day before Mount Vesuvius erupts, with devastating consequences, in 79 AD. Their arrival is spotted by a soothsayer, who reports back to the Sibylline Sisterhood and tells them 'the blue box' has arrived, which has been foretold in an ancient prophecy. The Doctor and Donna head back to the Tardis, but it has vanished. It has been sold to a man called Caecilius, who thinks it is a piece of modern art.

The pair visit the home of Caecilius, where the Doctor claims to be a man called Spartacus and tries to take the Tardis off his hands. Donna keeps dropping hints about the volcano but is interrupted by the arrival of chief augur, Lucius.

Caecilius's daughter Evelina collapses and is taken to her room, where Donna notices that part of her arm has turned to stone. Caecilius tells the Doctor how the local soothsayers are able to predict everything with complete accuracy. The Doctor visits the home of Lucius and discovers it is full of slabs of stone, which look like modern-day circuit boards.

The Doctor realises the circuit board is an energy converter, but then discovers Lucius's arm is also made of stone. The Time Lord manages to escape and an angry Lucius summons the Lord of the Mountain. The Doctor heads back to the home of Caecilius but a large rock creature appears. He gets everyone to throw water over the monster, which causes it to crumble.

Donna is kidnapped by the Sibylline Sisterhood. The Doctor heads to her rescue and finds that the Sisterhood's High Priestess is made of stone. There is an alien creature inside the priestess, which is turning her into a Pyrovile.

The Doctor realises the energy converter will prevent the eruption, by diverting power to the Pyroviles, who want to conquer Earth. He can save Earth, but only by destroying Pompeii. As Vesuvius erupts, there is pandemonium in the streets of Pompeii. The Doctor and Donna reach the Tardis in time, but Donna begs him to go back and save Caecilius and his family. The Doctor takes them to a hillside, where they see the destruction of the city. Later, Caecilius and his family start a new life in Rome.

Trivia and facts

The aliens in this story were originally called Pyrovillaxitrians, deriving from the Latin word 'pyro' meaning fire or heat. This was then shortened by writer James Moran to Pyrovillaxians and then Pyrovellians. Showrunner Russell T. Davies then removed another syllable to make the creatures the Pyroviles, who came from Pyrovillia.

After considering sites in Malta, Bulgaria and Rome, the production crew opted to use the backlot at Cinecitta Studios in Rome to recreate ancient Pompeii. The complex had been founded by Benito Mussolini in 1937 and was the home of classic movies like Ben Hur. Filming in Cinecitta Studios took place over two days - 13 September and 14 September 2007. The crew had a rest day on the Saturday, before flying back to the UK on 16 September 2007. Filming then resumed in Cardiff at the Temple of Peace a few days later.

The crew then returned to Clearwell Caves in Gloucestershire to film the scenes in the rock tunnel, the caves having previously been used in 'The Christmas Invasion' and 'The Impossible Planet/The Satan Pit'. Originally, the script indicated that after the Doctor exposed Lucius' arm he would smash it on the ground to destroy it, but David Tennant felt this was too cruel and asked for it to be toned down. Capaldi, who like Tennant is a lifelong Doctor Who fan, reportedly found seeing the Tardis for the first time on set 'very moving'.

'Planet of the Ood'

Original UK airdate: 19 April 2008
Cast: David Tennant as The Doctor, Catherine Tate as Donna Noble, Tim McInnerny as Mr Halpen, Ayesha Dharker as Solana Mercurio, Adrian Rawlins as Dr Ryder, Roger Griffiths as Commander Kess, Paul Clayton as Mr Bartle, Paul Kasey as Ood Sigma, Tariq Jordan as Rep and Silas Carson as the voice of the Ood
Written by Keith Temple
Directed by Graeme Harper
Music by Murray Gold
Produced by Susie Liggat
Filming dates: the main production ran from 21 August to 7 September 2007, with an additional filming day on 16 November
Running time: 43 minutes
Original UK viewing figures: 7.5 million

Review

Part-satire on the evils of corporate greed and part-polemic on the evils of slavery, 'Planet of the Ood' is a more sophisticated script than it first appears. At the time of broadcast, it was more noted for the return of the Ood, who had proved to have been so popular in the previous series that it was only a matter of time before they returned.

Instead of rehashing 'The Impossible Planet/The Satan Pit', this story expands Ood mythology and makes them far more interesting creatures. The mechanics of how they became slaves in the first place is properly addressed and once freed, they become more spiritual creatures. The episode also starts to drop subtle – well for Doctor Who anyway – hints about Donna Noble's possible fate.

The action scenes inside the warehouse are particularly good, and the story also gives Catherine Tate a chance to show more sides to Donna's character. There was criticism at the time that her casting would take the show in a more comedic direction, which was not exactly helped by the screwball antics in 'Partners in Crime', but the scene where Donna hears the Ood sing for the first time is really powerful. Doctor Who might not be considered proper drama, but it takes an actress of a certain calibre to tug on the heartstrings in that way.

Admittedly, you could see the twist about Mr Halpen coming a mile off, but it does cover a lot of ground for a single episode. It is one of the few times when the story might have benefitted from the luxury of being a two-parter.

The story
The Doctor and Donna arrive on a wintry planet, where they find an Ood, half-buried in the snow. The Ood cries out 'the circle must be broken' before dying. They then discover a large industrial complex, which is run by a company that sells Ood to various companies and interested buyers.

An alarm sounds out as a red-eyed Ood escapes from captivity and is hunted across the complex by armed guards. After gate-crashing a marketing reception, the Doctor and Donna decide to go 'off the beaten track' and break into one of the warehouses. They discover Ood packed into shipping containers and are spotted by the armed guards. First, Donna is captured and thrown into one of the shipping containers, containing more Ood. Then the guards capture the Doctor as well, but they escape after some Ood attack the guards.

As they walk through the complex, the Doctor starts to hear unprocessed Ood singing. He follows the telepathic song and finds a group of them cowering in a cage. He then allows Donna to hear them as well, but she is overcome by the sound.

The Doctor and Donna are then recaptured and brought in front of the chief executive of Ood Operations, Klineman Halpen. But then the Ood start revolting across the entire complex.

Halpen leaves the Doctor and Donna chained up in his office, but they are rescued by three Ood. One of the creatures, Ood Sigma, takes the Doctor and Donna to Warehouse 15, where they find a giant brain, which is a telepathic centre of the Ood hive mind. Halpen has set explosives around the brain, which are deactivated by the Doctor. Now free at least, the Ood can share their song. As they depart, Ood Sigma promises to include 'the-Doctor-Donna' in their song. He also warns the Doctor that his song must end soon.

Trivia and facts
The Ood proved to be so popular after they first appeared in 'The Impossible Planet/The Satan Pit' that showrunner Russell T. Davies had considered

bringing the Ood back in the previous season, with a consignment of the alien creatures hidden onboard the SS Pantallian in '42'.

At the tone meeting for the episode, the team were told to focus on the cinematic style of Ridley Scott, who directed such science fiction classics as Blade Runner and Alien, for the story.

The outdoor snow scenes were filmed in Trefil Quarry on the edge of the Brecon Beacons, which was also the location of the Vogsphere for the 2005 movie version of The Hitchhiker's Guide to the Galaxy. The Twin Peaks hangar on RAF St Athan in Barry was the location for the container warehouse scene, while additional filming also took place at Lafarge's Aberthaw Cement Works and Hensol Castle.

During the filming of the episode, the Royal Shakespeare Company (RSC) announced David Tennant would be re-joining them and take the lead in Hamlet, as part of its 2008 season. On 3 September 2007, the BBC issued a statement to follow up from the RSC's announcement.

After months of media speculation, the BBC can confirm that the BAFTA award-winning *Doctor Who* will return for the fifth series in Spring 2010. In 2009, Doctor Who will return with three specials starring David Tennant, with head-writer, Russell T. Davies.

On 31 August 2007, Tennant also travelled up with Julie Gardner to switch on Blackpool's illuminations, which included several *Doctor Who* items.

'The Sontaran Strategem/The Poison Sky'

Original UK airdate: 26 April/3 May 2008
Cast: David Tennant as The Doctor, Catherine Tate as Donna Noble, Freema Agyeman as Martha Jones, Billie Piper as Rose Tyler, Bernard Cribbins as Wilfred Mott, Jacqueline King as Sylvia Noble, Ryan Sampson as Luke Rattigan, Rupert Holliday Evans as Colonel Mace, Christopher Ryan as General Staal, Dan Starkey as Commander Skorr, Eleanor Matsuura as Jo Nakashima, Clive Standen as Private Harris, Wesley Theobald as Private Gray, Christian Cooke as Ross Jenkins, Rad Kaim as the Worker, Meryl Fernandes as the Female Student, Leeshon Alexander as the Male Student, Bridget Hodgson as Captain Price, Kirsty Wark as Herself, Lachele Carl as US Newsreader and Elizabeth Ryder as Atmos Voice
Written by Helen Raynor
Directed by Douglas Mackinnon
Music by Murray Gold
Produced by Susie Liggat
Filming dates: the main production ran from 23 October to 22 November 2007, with additional filming days on 5 and 18 December, 24 January and 29 February 2008
Running time: 44/44 minutes
Original UK viewing figures: 7/6.5 million

Review

The Sontarans were never exactly in the premier league of Doctor Who villains, despite being created by one of the classic series' foremost writers, Robert Holmes. Apart from a promising start in 1973's 'The Time Warrior' and 1975's 'The Sontaran Experiment', they quickly slipped back into obscurity and the less said about their final appearance in 1985's 'The Two Doctors', the better as it could easily win the award for the least convincing alien costumes in the history of television.

Bringing them back into the revived series was a courageous move. But it is to everyone's credit that the rebooted Sontarans were a vast improvement on the previous incarnation. Not only do they look far more convincing, but Helen Raynor establishes them as proper villains in their own right. They might be short, a bit thick and have potato heads, but they know how to fight, which is more than they ever did when they briefly landed in Seville back in the 1980s.

Elsewhere, the plot is fairly generic, using the well-worn plot device of brainwashed soldiers and evil doppelgangers, although kudos for tapping into the environmental zeitgeist with aliens wanting to exterminate humanity by polluting them to death.

There are lots of twists and action to keep the casual viewers happy and the return of one of the series most underrated characters, Martha Jones, which is never a bad thing. It might not be the darkest or the most dramatic story of the season. At times, it feels more like a comic book, with baddies you know will never win, but it's still good fun.

The story

The Doctor receives a call from former companion Martha Jones, who is now working for the Unified Intelligence Taskforce (UNIT).UNIT have raided a factory that makes the ATMOS (Atmospheric Omission System) devices for cars, searching for 'illegal aliens'. But their arrival is detected by an unseen group of aliens.

Colonel Mace is leading the investigation and tells the Doctor 52 people died at the same time around the world. They were all inside cars at the time fitted with ATMOS devices, which reduce all car emissions to zero. ATMOS has been developed by a young prodigy, Luke Rattigan, but UNIT suspects that alien technology may be involved. Deep in the factory, two UNIT soldiers are caught by a Sontaran, General Staal 'the undefeated', who brainwashes them.

Donna Noble goes hunting around the factory's personnel department and discovers nobody in the workforce has ever been ill. The Doctor visits the Rattigan Academy and meets Luke Rattigan himself. The Academy is full of advanced technology, including a teleport pod. Meanwhile, the brainwashed soldiers take Martha to a locked room, down in the depths of the factory. The room contains a Sontaran device, which allows the aliens to make a perfect clone of the Doctor's former companion. Staal orders his battle fleet to move to the final phase and all the ATMOS devices to be activated. All around the world, the devices start pouring out poisonous gas, choking everybody.

As chaos reigns, the cloned version of Martha secretly downloads NATO security protocols into her phone. The two brainwashed soldiers find the Tardis and teleport it up to the Sontaran spaceship. Unknown to them, Donna is onboard and now in space. UNIT launches nuclear missiles at the spaceship, but the Sontarans are one step ahead as Martha's clone cancels the launch using her mobile phone.

The Sontarans then invade the factory and quickly overcome the UNIT soldiers, but the flying aircraft carrier Valiant is called in and turns the tide. The Doctor heads into the basement of the factory and finds the real Martha.

The cloned Martha pulls a gun on the Doctor and says she was the one stopping the missile launch, but the Doctor overcomes her. The Doctor is able to get the teleport device in the laboratory working and he uses it to teleport to the Rattigan Academy, where he is able to use an atmospheric converter to burn away the Sontaran's gas and allow everyone to breathe again. With the skies clear again, General Staal orders his soldiers to prepare for all-out war. The Doctor teleports on their ship with the modified atmospheric converter and offers Staal a chance to leave the solar system. But then Luke Rattigan teleports the Doctor off the ship and swaps places with him. He activates the converter and destroys the Sontaran battle cruiser.

Back on the Tardis, Donna asks Martha if she would like to travel with the Doctor again, but before Martha can leave, the Tardis takes off with her on board.

Trivia and facts

Russell T. Davies' original idea for the story was that everyone in the country had new chimneys installed in their homes, which offered a way to clean the polluted atmosphere. But as writer Helen Raynor began to develop the script, the story took a new direction, which involved cars and satnav devices. Raynor was inspired by recent news stories where road traffic accidents had been blamed on the devices.

The original scripts also featured Donna Noble's father, Geoff, but by this point, it was clear that the actor who played him, Howard Attfield was extremely ill and would not be able to carry on filming. The scenes involving his character were then re-written and his lines given to Wilfred Mott, who first appeared in 'Voyage of the Damned' and was played by Bernard Cribbins.

All the Sontaran costumes were based on a body cast of Christopher Ryan, who played the aliens' leader, General Staal. This meant all the other actors who were in the costumes had to be between four foot ten inches and five foot two inches.

Although UNIT had returned to the rebooted series in 'Aliens of London/ World War Three', this was the first time that it is fully named. When UNIT was first introduced in the 1968 story 'The Invasion', it stood for the United Nations Intelligence Taskforce. For this two-parter, showrunner Russell T. Davis renamed it the Unified Intelligence Taskforce.

Margram County Park in Port Talbot was used as the location for Rattigan Academy, while a disused shampoo and hair conditioner factor on Usk Valley Business Park in Pontypool was used for the ATMOS factory. A day's filming also took place on Nant-Fawr Road in Cardiff, where all the scenes for the Noble household took place.

'The Doctor's Daughter'

Original UK airdate: 10 May 2008
Cast: David Tennant as The Doctor, Catherine Tate as Donna Noble, Freema Agyeman as Martha Jones, Georgia Moffett as Jenny, Nigel Terry as Cobb, Joe Dempsie as Cline, Paul Kasey as Hath Peck, Ruari Mears as Hath Gable, Akin Gazi as Carter and Olalekan Lawal Jr. as Soldier
Written by Stephen Greenhorn
Directed by Alice Troughton
Music by Murray Gold
Produced by Phil Collinson
Filming dates: the main production ran from 11 December to 21 December 2007, with a break for Christmas. It then ran from 7 January to 11 January 2008, with additional filming days on 18 and 24 January
Running time: 45 minutes
Original UK viewing figures: 7.3 million

Review

At some point, the producers of *Doctor Who* must have realised they could troll their own audience by coming up with titles and trailers that would literally send thousands of disbelieving fans into the unwelcoming arms of social media. 'The Doctor's Daughter' is a prime example. Not only was Jennie played by the daughter of the Fifth Doctor, Peter Davison, but she was the daughter of the lead character. How on Earth could this happen, they wailed on the online forums, conveniently ignoring the fact that the Doctor has a granddaughter, Susan Foreman, who travelled with the Time Lord in the early days of the series.

Anyone hoping for a revelation about the Doctor's other siblings, or even Susan Foreman, which in itself is claimed every five minutes on Twitter by someone who has 'inside knowledge', was always going to be disappointed. The production team quickly batted that one away by firmly establishing that Jennie had been artificially created by using a tissue sample from the Doctor all before the opening credits.

What follows is a more by-the-numbers science fiction tale of two armies locked in a perpetual stalemate, until the Doctor arrives. There are shades of the endless war between the Thals and the Kaleds in the Fourth Doctor classic 'Genesis of the Daleks'. What elevates 'The Doctor's Daughter' over the regular nonsense is the twist at the end, which I would defy anyone to see coming. The revelation that the war itself is only seven days old is a corker, even if it stretches credibility somewhat.

Sadly, Jennie never appeared in the series again, which feels like a missed opportunity, particularly as Georgia Moffett really nails the part. At least she got her own spin-off with Big Finish, which is worth investigating. Even without the trolling, this is still a decent adventure.

The story

The Tardis crash lands in a dark tunnel, and the Doctor is captured by soldiers, who put his hand into a machine that takes tissue samples. Seconds later, a young woman steps out of the machine, who has been created using the Time Lord's tissue. She is the Doctor's daughter. The young woman takes up arms and fights with the soldiers, as they come under fire from an alien race, known as the Hath. One of these creatures takes Martha away. The young woman then blows up the tunnel, trapping Martha on the other side.

Martha uses her medical skills to help the injured Hath soldiers. Meanwhile, Donna christens the young woman Jenny as they are led to meet General Cobb.

He tells them they have been at war with the Hath for many years. He explains his ancestors came to this planet to build a new colony, but the Hath wanted it for themselves. Both sides are also looking for something called 'the Source', which Cobb says is the 'breath of life'. The Doctor inadvertently reveals the location to both the humans and the Hath, who appear to have identical copies of the same map.

Both sides start preparing for a massive battle. As the war begins, Martha takes one of the Hath above ground, while the Doctor, Donna and Jenny search for 'the Source'. As they walk around, Donna notices there are numbers on the walls, which appear to be counting down.

On the surface, Martha slips into a bubbling pit. She is saved by her Hath companion, who sacrifices himself to get her out of the pit. She eventually finds the temple containing 'the Source' from the surface, just as the Doctor, Donna and Jenny enter it through a hidden tunnel. They realise the temple is actually the spaceship, which brought the humans ancestors to the planet. Martha realises the significance of the numbers on all the walls – they represent the date they were built. It has only been seven days since the war broke out.

The humans and the Hath have created so many generations through their tissue sample machines - up to twenty per day - that their own history has quickly become a myth, getting more distorted as it gets passed on.

Both sides burst into the temple, and the Doctor explains that 'the Source' is just a terraforming device, used to make barren planets habitable again.

The Doctor declares the war is over and he smashes the device onto the ground, allowing it to begin rebuilding the planet. Cobb tries to shoot the Doctor, but Jenny takes the bullet instead and then dies in his arms. The Tardis departs and returns to Earth. Martha says she has had enough and leaves the Doctor and Donna to travel on their own. Elsewhere, the body of Jenny is being prepared for her funeral when she comes back to life. Jenny then steals a rocket and heads out into the universe on her own.

Trivia and facts

On the episode's DVD commentary, Russell T. Davies describes 'The Doctor's Daughter' as 'the toughest brief we've ever given a writer'. As well as the title itself, the shopping list given to Stephen Greenhorn included a subterranean war, the Hath and an unpleasant experience for Martha Jones, which would make her want to return home at the end of the story. The original plan was that the story should also conclude with the death of Jenny, but that was changed after Steven Moffat suggested that she shouldn't die, as that was what the audience would be expecting.

Georgia Moffett had been put forward for the role of Rose Tyler in 2004 and then auditioned for a part in 'The Unicorn and the Wasp', before being considered for this episode. After filming the 'Time Crash' for Children in Need, Moffett's father, the Fifth Doctor Peter Davison phoned her and said: 'Right. That's it. It's your go.'

The read-through took place at Bloomsbury Baptist Church in London on 23 November 2007. Before it took place, Davies paid tribute to Verity Lambert, the original producer of Doctor Who, who had died the previous evening.

An open cast colliery at Aberbaiden, near Kenfig, was used as the filming location for the hostile terrain of Messaline. The Marble Room in City Hall, Cardiff was used as the Hath Encampment, while the Dupont Building on the Mamhilad Industrial Park in Pontypool functioned as a spaceship corridor. The final venue for the story was the Barry Shooting Range in Barry Island, where a disused railway tunnel, which had been turning into a shooting gallery, was also utilised.

'The Unicorn and the Wasp'

Original UK airdate: 17 May 2008
Cast: David Tennant as The Doctor, Catherine Tate as Donna Noble, Fenella Woolgar as Agatha Christie, Felicity Kendal as Lady Eddison, Tom Goodman-Hill as Reverend Golightly, Christopher Benjamin as Colonel Hugh, Felicity Jones as Robina Redmond, Adam Rayner as Roger Curbishley, David Quilter as Greeves, Daniel King as Davenport, Ian Barritt as Professor Peach, Leena Dhingra as Miss Chandrakala, Charlotte Eaton as Mrs Hart, Daphne Oxenford as Old Agatha and Natalie Barrett as the Nurse
Written by Gareth Roberts
Directed by Graeme Harper
Music by Murray Gold
Produced by Susie Liggat
Filming dates: the main production ran from 8 August to 21 August 2007, with additional filming days on 6 and 7 September, and 16 November
Running time: 45 minutes
Original UK viewing figures: 7.3 million

Review

Having already established himself as one of *Doctor Who's* more literary writers with 'The Shakespeare Code', Gareth Roberts turned his attention to another legendary author, Agatha Christie. Taking inspiration from a real-life incident when Ms Christie went missing for eleven days in 1926, prompting a nationwide search, Roberts wastes no time in using every cliché in the whodunnit book to pay a knowing tribute to the prolific author. That said, as Christie purists will point out, the author actually vanished in December 1926, while this episode clearly takes place in the summer.

There are a country house, a jewel thief and family secrets. There's also a war hero, a country vicar and a debutante. There's even a murder in the library with lead piping, for crying out loud. The only thing that is missing is a diminutive Belgian and a Cluedo board.

It's best not to take the episode too seriously. Just sit back and enjoy the ride. The revelation about the giant wasp is almost as preposterous as some of Christie's own denouements. The scene where the characters give their alibis, intercut with what they were really doing, is one of the finest ever send-ups of the genre.

'The Unicorn and the Wasp' is Doctor Who as an out-and-out farce, but if you have ever had to endure the endless repeats on Miss Marple and Poirot, then at least you can amuse yourself by ticking off all the Agatha Christie references. And there are quite a few.

The story

The Doctor and Donna materialise in front of a large country house in the roaring '20s. The house is home to Lady Clemency Eddison and she is holding a party for some of her friends. Suitably dressed for the occasion, the Doctor and Donna head for the lawn, where cocktails are being served. The other guests include Lady Eddison's husband, Colonel Hugh Curbishley, the Reverend Golightly and the crime writer Agatha Christie.

The Doctor confides to Donna that it is 1926 and Christie is about to vanish for ten days, before turning up in a hotel in Harrogate with no memory of what had happened to her. She never talked about or explained the incident. But the bonhomie is short-lived when the body of Professor Peach is found in the library. The Doctor and Agatha Christie start investigating the murder, and the Doctor finds some morphic residue around the body. Meanwhile, Donna heads upstairs and finds a locked door. The butler Greeves explains to her that Lady Eddison spent six months in the room after returning from India with malaria. Then she sees a giant wasp outside, which smashes through the window and attacks her.

The wasp then vanishes, leaving the Doctor to suspect it may be one of the houseguests in disguise. The Doctor realises he has been poisoned with cyanide and races to the kitchen, where he cures himself with a combination of ginger beer, anchovies and a big shock – which turned out to be a kiss from Donna.

Later that night, over dinner, the Doctor tells the other guests he has laced the soup with pepper, which contains an active ingredient used in insecticide. The lights go out and the giant wasp re-appears. Chaos ensures and Lady Eddison's son, Roger is found dead, with a knife in his back.

The remaining guests gather together and Christie deduces that Robina Redmond has stolen Lady Eddison's precious Firestone. The Doctor deduces that the Reverend Golightly is, in fact, Lady Eddison's son, who was born out of wedlock in India. The Firestone is a telepathic recorder and the Reverend is the murderer. He transforms into a wasp and flies off. The Doctor, Donna and Christie give chase and catch up with him at Silent Pool Lake. Donna throws the Firestone into the water and the wasp dives in and drowns. Christie collapses and suffers from a bout of amnesia. Ten days later, she wakes up in a hotel in Harrogate with no memory of what actually happened.

Trivia and facts
In the early stages of development, writer Gareth Roberts toyed with whether to use a young Agatha Christie or an older version of the celebrated crime novelist, with her acting like one of her most famous creations, Miss Marple. In the end, they settled for 1926, when the young writer went missing for several days, before being discovered in Harrogate. No definite reason for her behaviour was ever given.

The 'wasp' in the title was inspired by an illustration by Tom Adams, which adorned the cover of certain editions of Christie's 1935 Hercule Poirot mystery Death in the Clouds. Christie's grandson, Mathew Prichard attended the first reading of the script. Davies told Doctor Who Magazine:

It's the best seal of approval we could ever hope for.

Llansannor Court in the Vale of Glamorgan, which previously appeared as Torchwood House in '*Tooth and Claw*', was used for the external scenes and many of the internal scenes at Eddison Hall. David Tennant's father, the former Reverend Sandy McDonald, who was staying with his son in Wales at the time of filming, played a footman in some of these scenes. Other Eddison Hall internal scenes were shot at Tredegar House in Newport and Upper Boat Studios. A night shoot was also held at Hensol Castle, which is just outside Cardiff.

The story was due to finish with a scene set in 1976 when the Doctor and Donna visit an elderly Agatha Christie and present her with a copy of Death in the Clouds, complete with a giant wasp on the cover. 'Although it was a lovely sequence, it just seemed unnecessary,' commented director Graeme Harper in the podcast commentary, which was released online after the episode was originally broadcast.

'Silence in the Library/Forest of the Dead'
Original UK airdate: 31 May/7 June 2008
Cast: David Tennant as The Doctor, Catherine Tate as Donna Noble, Alex Kingston

as Professor River Song, Colin Salmon as Dr Moon, Eve Newton as The Girl, Mark Dexter as Dad, Sarah Niles as Node 1, Joshua Dallas as Node 2, Jessika Williams as Anita, Steve Pemberton as Strackman Lux, Talulah Riley as Miss Evangelista, O-T Fagbenie as Other Dave, Harry Peacock as Proper Dave, Jason Pitt as Lee, Eloise Rakic-Platt as Ella, Alex Midwood as Joshua and Jonathan Reuben as the Man
Written by Steven Moffat
Directed by Euros Lyn
Music by Murray Gold
Produced by Phil Collinson
Filming dates: the main production ran from 15 January to 14 February 2008, with additional filming days on 19 and 20 March
Running time: 43/45 minutes
Original UK viewing figures: 6.2/7.8 million

Review

The return of Steven Moffat to *Doctor Who* is always a cause for celebration and having delivered the incredible 'Blink' in the last series, expectations were high for 'Silence in the Library/Forest of the Dead'. Like Moffat's best work, the two-parter is fiendishly complicated. If you turn away from the screen for just one minute, you will be completely and utterly lost. Moffat also replicates a bit of 'Blink's' success by coming up with a villain that can be found in everyday life. Last time around, it was killer statues. Now he gives us deadly shadows, and I'm not talking about Hank Marvin.

Alex Kingston makes a huge impression as Professor River Song. It's little wonder that Moffat brought her back in the Eleventh Doctor era although her storyline got increasingly complex with every appearance. The Moffat template of strong women, who can tug at the Doctor's heartstrings has been already established in 'The Girl in the Fireplace'. But you really get the impression that Professor Song has known the Doctor for a long time, and watching it again after these years, you cannot help but marvel at how seamlessly this sits alongside her later appearances.

It also boasts one of the finest cliffhangers of the season, with a genuine 'how will they get out of that?' moment. The second half also requires a fair bit of concentration as Moffat brings all the various plot strands together. You are left thinking what might have been if David Tennant had stuck around for one more series under Moffat. No disrespect to Matt Smith, but 'Silence in the Library/Forest of the Dead' is one of this era's scariest scripts.

The story

A little girl dreams of being alone in a giant library, where she can fly around, but suddenly two other people appear in the building – the Doctor and Donna.

Meanwhile, the Tardis materialises on a planet known simply as The Library, which the Doctor tells Donna is the largest in the universe. The Doctor is surprised to find the whole planet is deserted.

An information node with a human face tells the pair that the library has sealed itself and to 'count the shadows if you want to be safe'. The Doctor and Donna run into another large room, where they find a security camera, which appears to be linked to the little girl seen at the beginning of the episode. A team of explorers then enter the same room. They are led by the archaeologist Professor River Song and financed by businessman Strackman Lux, whose grandfather originally built the library. The Doctor tells them to avoid the shadows and stay in the light. The library has been invaded by a deadly species called the Vashta Nerada, which exists in the dark.

The Professor clearly knows who the Doctor is and brings out a battered blue book. One of the crew tries to access the library computer system, but instead, a telephone rings in the little girl's house, which only she can hear. Lux's secretary Miss Evangelista is attacked by the Vashta Nerada, which reduce her to a skeleton. The rest of them flee for their lives through the library corridors, until the Doctor spots another information node with Donna's face. 'Donna Noble has been saved,' it tells him.

The little girl is sitting at home, watching the Doctor and the crew run from the Vashta Nerada in the library. She then changes the channel and sees Donna arrive at a hospital called CAL, where she is tended by the mysterious Dr Moon. At the hospital, she meets a man called Lee. They get married and have two children. Back in the library, the Professor produces a future version of the Doctor's sonic screwdriver. 'One day, I'm going to be someone you trust completely,' she tells him, before whispering something in his ear.

Lux tells the crew the moon in the sky is a virus checker called 'Dr Moon', which supports the computer in the planet's core. In her reality, Donna meets a woman dressed all in black, who is Miss Evangelista. She tells her they have both been saved in the library's computer. The Vashta Nerada tell the Doctor they came from the forests that were used to create all the books in the library. The Doctor then realises all the books are backed up on the library's data core.

Lux says the computer's main command node is called CAL, named after his grandfather's youngest daughter, Charlotte Abigail Lux. The little girl was dying, so her mind was uploaded to the mainframe, with Dr Moon to look after her.

The girl saved everyone in the library from the Vashta Nerada, but the Doctor reasons she is now running out of memory space. The Vashta Nerada agree to give the Doctor one day to free all the people trapped in the computer core.

So, he tries to hook himself up to the computer, but the Professor knocks him out and takes his place. As the computer resets, the Professor dies, but everyone in the computer, including Donna, return to the library. The Doctor remembers the future screwdriver. It contains a copy of Professor River Song and plugs it into the computer. The Professor wakes up in the hospital and is greeted by the little girl and Dr Moon, along with her former colleagues.

Trivia and facts

Writer Steven Moffat first suggested the idea of a *Doctor Who* story set in a library back in 2004, after he had completed his two scripts for the first series with Christopher Eccleston. The original idea involved strange windows connecting all the libraries from the past. In the early stages of development, it was a little boy rather than a little girl controlling the library. The gender was changed because it was felt that a girl was more vulnerable. Moffatt wrote the first episode while he was also working on the first draft of the movie *The Adventures of Tintin*, which was released in 2011 and directed by Steven Spielberg. Donna's children were originally called Alan and Tracy but were later renamed Joshua, after Moffat's own son and Ella, after one of his son's friends.

Hensol Castle in the Vale of Glamorgan, which had appeared in several other episodes, was used to film the hospital scenes, while Dyffryn Gardens was the location for some of the hospital grounds scenes. Swansea Library on Alexandra Road was used as another filming location. The building had been standing empty since November 2007 after its contents had been transferred to a new library. Coincidentally, Euros Lyn and Helen Raynor had studied there for their exams when they were students.

On 24 January 2008, the BBC issued a press release confirming that both Alex Kingston and Colin Salmon had joined the cast for the two-part story. Kingston said in the press release:

> I used to watch Doctor Who through the crack in the door, I was so terrified, but I couldn't tear myself away. I loved it so much and I'm so delighted to be part of the new series.

The second episode went through many titles, including 'River's Run'and 'Forest of the Night', before the production team and Moffat settled on 'Forest of the Dead'.

'Midnight'

Original UK airdate: 14 June 2008
Cast: David Tennant as The Doctor, Catherine Tate as Donna Noble, Billie Piper as Rose Tyler, Lesley Sharp as Sky Sylvestry, Rakie Ayola as Hostess, David Troughton as Professor Hobbes, Ayesha Antoine as Dee Dee Blasco, Lindsey Coulson as Val Cane, Daniel Ryan as Biff Cane, Colin Morgan as Jethro Cane, Tony Bluto as Drive Joe and Duane Henry as Mechanic Claude
Written by Russell T. Davies
Directed by Alice Troughton
Music by Murray Gold
Produced by Phil Collinson
Filming dates: the main production ran from 27 November to 11 December 2007
Running time: 43minutes
Original UK viewing figures: 8 million

Review

Throughout Russell T. Davies' tenure as showrunner, there are plenty of episodes and moments where the action is played very broadly, almost as if it was torn from the pages of a Marvel comic book. That is not necessarily a bad thing. *Doctor Who* should always be exciting, fast-paced and fun. And while at times, the Tenth Doctor's era could be defined as too romantic, melodramatic or just plain silly, there are also some genuinely dark and scary moments.

'Midnight' is as dark as Russell T. Davies gets and after re-watching it all these years later, you cannot help but appreciate just how unsettling it really is. We've seen the Doctor triumph time and time again, and always defying the odds. This is a story where the Time Lord is overwhelmed by a particular set of circumstances and if it were not for the intervention of the Hostess, he would have lost. Nobody wants the hero to be completely infallible, but likewise, no one really wants to see the beloved Doctor as vulnerable as this.

'Midnight' takes a lot of risks, but the small cast and the claustrophobic set give it a real edge. Lesley Sharp's performance as the possessed Sky Sylvestry is particularly noteworthy. The moment when the Doctor and Sky start talking in unison is a serious contender for one of the series most disturbing moments. Despite the similarities in plot, 'Midnight' is the polar opposite of 'Voyage of the Damned'. One is fun and games, the other is chilling. The survivors do not band together, they slowly turn on each other. You would not want a whole series of episodes like this and it's definitely too dark for younger audiences. You may want to watch a lighter episode after this one, just to restore balance in the time vortex.

The story

The Doctor takes Donna to the diamond planet of Midnight. As she relaxes at a spa, he decides to take a trip to see its famous sapphire waterfalls. Onboard the Crusader 50, he meets the other passengers, including Professor Hobbes and his researcher Dee Dee Blasco and a middle-aged woman travelling on her own, Sky Silvestry.

The cruiser's entertainment system fails, so the passengers get to know each other. But as the journey progresses, the cruiser comes to a halt. The Hostess says it is just a short delay and the Doctor heads to the cockpit to investigate. Everything appears to be working but the ship is not moving.

He heads back to the rest of the passengers and tells them everything is being sorted out. Then everyone hears two loud thumps on the side of the ship. Then there are another two on the other side. Sky starts to behave oddly, screaming: 'It's coming for me'. Then she sits on the floor, starts repeating everything all the other passengers are saying. Then she starts to repeat only what the Doctor is saying. The Doctor thinks the entity outside is trying to communicate to them through Sky.

As they talk, Sky starts to say everything the Doctor says at the same time, leading the other passengers to think the entity has also possessed the Time

Lord as well. Suddenly, Sky can move again, but the Doctor appears to be paralysed.

Sky urges the other passengers to throw the Doctor out of the craft, but the hostess realises she is still possessed. As the other passengers grab the Doctor, she takes Sky, opens the door, and they are both sucked outside.

Trivia and facts

The eighth episode of this series was originally going to be written by Tom MacRae, who penned 'Rise of the Cybermen/The Age of Steel' in the second series. MacRae's script was titled 'Century House' and saw the Doctor joining the line-up of a 'Most Haunted' style television show to track down the ghost of the Red Widow.

As work progressed on the fourth series, it was decided that 'Century House' was too similar to another story, which had also been commissioned, 'The Unicorn and the Wasp'.

Instead, showrunner Russell T. Davies decided to write a replacement in the four days before the director joined the team for pre-production in October. The bulk of the script comprised just one scene, with scene nine running for 44 of the 60 pages. Sam Kelly, who was perhaps better known for his roles in *'Allo 'Allo!* and *Porridge* was originally cast in the role of Professor Hobbes. Unfortunately, Kelly was involved in a car accident and broke his leg, which meant the part had to be recast days before the script read-through.

The role then went to David Troughton, who as well as being the son of the Second Doctor, Patrick Troughton, also had a long history with the show, having appeared in the 1967/8 story 'The Enemy of the World', 1969's 'The War Games' and 1972's 'The Curse of Peladon'. Troughton told Radio Times:

I was rung up with two days' notice to go to Cardiff, 'I wrote to Sam: 'Promise it wasn't me'. It's not very nice getting a job in that way, but the show must go on.

Despite having the same surname, David Troughton and director Alice Troughton are not related. The recording of 'Midnight' occurred completely in sequence and to add to the sense of claustrophobia, the cast were ferried from their hotel before dawn's first light and were returned back after night had fallen.

'Turn Left'

Original UK airdate: 21 June 2008
Cast: David Tennant as The Doctor, Catherine Tate as Donna Noble, Billie Piper as Rose Tyler, Bernard Cribbins as Wilfred Mott, Jacqueline King as Sylvia Noble, Joseph Long as Rocco Colasanto, Noma Dumezweni as Capt. Magambo, Chipo Chung as Fortune Teller, Marcia Lecky as Mooky Kahari, Suzann McLean as Veena Brady, Natalie Walter as Alice Coltrane, Neil Clench as Man in Pub, Clive Standen as

UNIT Soldier, Bhasker Patel as Jival Chowdry
Written by Russell T. Davies
Directed by Graeme Harper
Music by Murray Gold
Produced by Susie Liggat
Filming dates: the main production ran from 22 November to 8 December 2007, with additional filming days on 18/24 and 31 January, and 20 March 2008
Running time: 49 minutes
Original UK viewing figures: 8 million

Review

Having proved he can do dark and depressing with the previous episode, 'Midnight', Russell T. Davies shows us another side to his oeuvre by writing something that is really dark and depressing. Cheap jokes aside, 'Turn Left' uses the well-worn concept of alternative realities to explore the character of Donna Noble, as well as reusing key scenes from previous series. The Doctor is now dead and life for everyone on Earth, including his future companion, will never be the same again. It also heralds the proper return of Rose Tyler, who has been creeping up in the background throughout the series.

Russell T. Davies' vision of a world without the Doctor is truly terrifying. Previous victories become defeats and society as we know it swiftly collapses, with internment camps, martial law and food shortages. There's even a dead Tardis. It rapidly becomes the Doctor Who equivalent of the once seen, never forgotten 1980s nuclear war horror film Threads, except it was all filmed in Wales. Be thankful Brexit was not 'a thing' back then or else he might have chucked that in too, just for good measure, although Rocco Colasanto's line about 'England being for the English' now seems oddly prophetic.

The showrunner does lay it on a bit thick at times. It seems a bit harsh that Leeds becomes a dumping ground for displaced Londoners. What did Leeds ever do to deserve that? But at least it gives Bernard Cribbins and Catherine Tate a chance to get stuck into some meaty scenes and act their socks off. And just when you thought things could not get any worse, they do. Having gone through hell and back, the alternative Donna dies in the middle of a road. Quite what she did in Russell T. Davies' imagination to warrant such an end is anyone's guess, although the fate awaiting her in the finale is even worse...

Best of all, it ends on a terrific cliffhanger. Davies might have just served up two of the darkest episodes in the show's history, but the sight of the Tenth Doctor running into the market and seeing all the 'Bad Wolf' signs shows us he hasn't lost any of his sparkle.

The story

As the Doctor and Donna walk through the bustling market streets of Shan Shen, the companion spots a fortune teller, who offers her a reading. Inside the parlour, Donna tells the fortune-teller of a fateful morning when she had to choose between a job at HC Clements and another, while out driving with her mother Sylvia. At a road junction, Donna turns the car left to go the interview at HC Clements.

Suddenly, a beetle appears on Donna's back and she is transported to an alternate reality where she turned right, did not take the HC Clements and never met the Doctor. In this reality, key scenes from previous episodes are replayed with very different endings. The Doctor was able to defeat the Empress of the Racnoss ('The Runaway Bride') but it cost him his life. As UNIT soldiers take his body away, Donna also meets a mysterious young woman who was 'just passing by'. Unknown to Donna, that young person is Rose Tyler.

The Royal Hope Hospital vanishes ('Smith and Jones') and when it returns, the news reports that a trainee doctor called Martha Jones was killed, along with a woman called Sarah Jane Smith. The Titanic then crashes into Buckingham Palace ('Voyage of the Dammed'), leaving millions of people dead. Martial law is declared, with non-British citizens placed in internment camps.

One night, Donna notices that the stars in the sky are going out. Rose appears again and tells Donna that the fabric of reality is collapsing. The stars in every reality are collapsing, and the Doctor is the only one who can save them. The two women travel to a UNIT base, where soldiers have rigged up a device using the Tardis to reveal the creature on Donna's back. Donna is sent back in time and told to make sure her earlier self turns left at that road junction.

She arrives with just four minutes to spare and rushes to warn her earlier self but gets knocked over by a van, causing a traffic jam. As Donna lies there dying, Rose appears again and whispers two words in her ear. The jam causes the earlier Donna to turn left and take the job at HC Clements. Normality is restored and Donna wakes up in the fortune teller's shop and the beetle falls off her back.

The Doctor arrives, and she tells him about the blonde woman, the stars going out and the two words the girl whispered to her – 'Bad Wolf'. Outside, the market is full of signs that now contain those same two words. The Doctor races back into the Tardis and hears the sound of the cloister bell ringing. 'It's the end of the universe,' he says.

Trivia and facts

Partly inspired by the 1998 film *Sliding Doors*, which followed two alternative lives for the same woman, 'Turn Left' was originally devised for Penny, who was going to be the companion before it was confirmed that Catherine Tate would return as Donna Noble. The initial idea was based on Penny driving into her estate with her mother, Moira, but would have turned right instead of left, and so would never have met the Doctor.

The fortune teller was played by Chipo Chung, who appeared beneath prosthetics in the previous year's 'Utopia' as the alien Chantho. Ben Righton also reprised his role as medical student Oliver Morgenstein from the episode

'Smith and Jones'. The fortune teller's set was built on the vault sets for the Torchwood Hub, which were not being used at the time.

The T-junction where Donna makes her fateful decision is located on Court Road in Gwan Tredoa, which was renamed Little Sutton Street by the crew. Marianne Hemming doubled for Catherine Tate behind the wheel of Donna's Peugeot 307 because Tate did not drive. The Maltings, near Cardiff Royal Infirmary and Splott Market, was used to create the exotic alien marketplace and Machen Street and Rudry Street in Penarth were used to film the terraced street in Leeds.

'The Stolen Earth/Journey's End'

Original UK airdate: 28 June/5 July 2008
Cast: David Tennant as The Doctor, Catherine Tate as Donna Noble, Freema Agyeman as Martha Jones, John Barrowman as Captain Jack Harkness, Elisabeth Sladen as Sarah Jane Smith, Billie Piper as Rose Tyler, Penelope Wilton as Harriet Jones, Noel Clarke as Mickey Smith, Camille Coduri as Jackie Tyler, Adjoa Andoh as Francine Jones, Eve Miles as Gwen Cooper, Gareth David-Lloyd as Ianto Jones, Thomas Knight as Luke Smith, Bernard Cribbins as Wilfred Mott, Jacqueline King as Sylvia Noble, Julian Bleach as Davros, Michael Brandon as General Sanchez, Andrea Harris as Suzanne, Lachele Carl as Trinity Wells, Barnaby Edwards, Nicholas Pegg, David Hankinson and Anthony Spargo as Dalek operators, Nicholas Briggs as the voice of the Daleks, John Leeson as the voice of K-9 and Alexander Armstrong as the voice of Mr Smith
Written by Russell T. Davies
Directed by Graeme Harper
Music by Murray Gold
Produced by Phil Collinson
Filming dates: the main production ran from 18 February to 31 March 2008, with additional filming days on 31 January and 1 May
Running time: 45/63minutes
Original UK viewing figures: 8.7/10.5 million

Review

By the time of the fourth *Doctor Who* series, viewers had come to get expect big finales with the stakes raised to 'end of the universe' proportions. The first half of this series finale does not disappoint for that reason. Russell T. Davies chucks everything but the kitchen sink at the all-action plot, with every spin-off character from the revived show returning for good measure. It rapidly becomes a comic book feast, with characters delivering lines like 'We are declaring ultimate code red!' with all the melodrama that such dialogue deserves. Rose Tyler even gets to strut around with a great big gun. If filmmaker Michael Bay ever gets his hands on *Doctor Who*, and let's pray he never does, then it would look an awful lot like 'The Stolen Earth'.

The return of the Daleks and, more importantly, their creator Davros makes perfect sense, although they seem to conquer the Earth remarkably quickly. Clearly, ultimate code red is not all it's cracked up to be. Having the Tenth Doctor regenerate at the end of 'The Stolen Earth' takes trolling the audience to a whole new level. It's one of the most audacious cliff hangers in the history of the programme, even if viewers would go 'huh?' when everything was explained the following week.

By the second half, there are an awful lot of characters and plot points to keep in the air. Davros, who was brilliantly played by Julian Bleach, rants something about a reality bomb, which presumably is a very bad thing. A duplicate Doctor gets created out of a Tenth Doctor's hand, which was chopped off back in the 'The Christmas Invasion', so Rose Tyler can live happily ever after in her parallel universe. And then there's poor Donna Noble, who becomes a Time Lord/human hybrid and ends up getting her mind wiped. If this finale is supposed to be a victory lap for the Tenth Doctor, then it ends on quite a downer, with the Tenth Doctor standing alone in the Tardis. It might not make a lot of sense at times, but there's no denying the epic nature of this finale.

The story

The Tardis materialises on Earth, and the Doctor and Donna rush out, only to find that it is just another ordinary Saturday morning. They head back inside the Doctor's ship, but seconds later the ground outside starts to shake. The Doctor opens the Tardis doors again and finds they are suddenly floating in space. The Tardis is in exactly the same place. The Earth itself has vanished.

In New York, Martha Jones is in the UNIT base.

In Cardiff, Captain Jack Harkness is with the Torchwood team.

In Bannerman Road, Sarah Jane Smith is with her son Luke.

One by one, they all look up in the sky, which is now full of 26 alien planets.

Rose Tyler then appears on Earth. Sarah's computer Mr Smith detects spaceships heading towards Earth. UNIT has also spotted the ships and declares a Code Red. The ships start to send a signal down to Earth. It is the sound of Daleks chanting 'Exterminate! Exterminate! Exterminate!'.

Former Prime Minister Harriet Jones activates the Subwave Network and contacts Sarah, Torchwood and Martha Jones. The call is also picked up by Donna's grandfather, Wilf Noble and Rose is able to listen in. Using the network, Harriet is able to contact the Doctor, who locates the Earth, one second in the future in the Medusa Cascade. But the Daleks also detect the network and exterminate Harriet.

The Doctor makes contact with Torchwood, Sarah and Martha, but another voice interrupts their conversation. It is Davros, the creator of the Daleks. He was rescued by Dalek Caan, who was part of the Cult of Skaro and has created a new race of Dalek from cells from his own body.

Mr Smith detects the Tardis landing and Sarah heads off to investigate. On a deserted street, the Doctor and Donna step out of the Tardis. At the end of the street, Rose Tyler is standing, waiting for the Tardis. They run towards each other, but before they can be reunited, a Dalek suddenly appears and blasts the Doctor. The Time Lord falls to the ground. Captain Jack appears and destroys the Dalek. He then helps Rose and Donna carry the injured Doctor back into the Tardis. In the Tardis, the Doctor starts to regenerate. The Doctor channels all his regeneration energy into his spare hand, which was cut off by the Sycorax in 'The Christmas Invasion'. The Daleks locate the Tardis and teleport it onboard the Crucible.

Mickey Smith and Jackie Tyler appear on Earth and save Sarah from the Daleks. The Doctor, Jack and Rose step out of the Tardis, while Donna remains inside. The Daleks remove the Tardis and drop it into the core of the Crucible where it is torn apart.

Trapped inside the Tardis, Donna reaches out to the glass jar that contains the Doctor's spare hand. Regeneration energy starts to flow out of the hand and a body appears. It is a cloned version of the Doctor, albeit a naked one. The cloned Doctor explains that he was created by a biological metacrisis and is part Doctor and part Donna. Mickey, Jackie and Sarah are all brought onboard the Crucible.

The real Doctor and Rose are taken to the Crucible's vault, where they meet Davros, who says the Daleks plan to use a reality bomb to destroy the entire universe. Only the Daleks themselves will survive. The Tardis materialises in the vault and the cloned Doctor and Donna emerge. Davros blasts Donna with electricity, which triggers another biological metacrisis. Suddenly, she has all of the Doctor's knowledge and is able to take control of the Daleks, defeat Davros and return all the planets to their rightful places.

As the Crucible explodes, all the companions run into the Tardis. They then use it to drag the Earth back to its original position.

Back on Earth, the Doctor leaves Mickey and Martha with Jack and then returns to the parallel universe with Rose and Jackie. He leaves the cloned Doctor with Rose, who can grow old with her. In the Tardis, Donna starts to become overwhelmed with the Time Lord knowledge in her head and breaks down. The Doctor is forced to wipe all her memories of him in order to save her. He then leaves her unconscious with her mother Sylvia and Wilf and bids them goodbye.

Trivia and facts

While writing the scripts for this two-part episode, Russell T. Davies kept playing the Paul and Linda McCartney song 'Live and Let Die', which was the theme to the 1973 James Bond movie of the same name. Davies originally planned to kill off one of the companions. He knew that he could not kill off Rose and producer Phil Collinson told him they could not kill off Mickey, either.

The showrunner also hoped to bring back Russell Tovey as Midshipman Frame, who had appeared in 'Voyage of the Damned'. However, Tovey was appearing in

The Sea at the Theatre Royal Haymarket in London and was unavailable.

Davros was referred to as 'Enemy D' in a bid to keep his return a secret. While lifelong Doctor Who fan Tennant immediately understood the significance of bringing back the character of Davros, Tate was less excited. 'I didn't know who Davros was,' she later admitted on BBC1's The Graham Norton Show. 'And for a brief second, I thought they meant Stavros, Harry Enfield's character.'

Filming started on 18 February 2008 with the Tardis scenes at Upper Boat Studios.

David Tennant's regular double Colum Sanson-Regan, in a matching suit and haircut, was used for the shots requiring two Doctors. The Shadow Architect scenes were filmed at the School of Optometry and Visual Sciences in Cardiff University, and the production team returned to Southerndown Beach for the Bad Wolf Bay scenes. The long-awaited reunion scenes for the Doctor and Rose were shot on the streets of Penarth. Rose arrived on Queens Road, Jack first appeared on Arcot Street, and the Doctor was shot down by a Dalek on the intersection of Paget Road and Queens Road. Rose saved Wilf and Sylvia from the Daleks in neighbouring Plantagenet Street.

The final scene of Journey's End showed a group of Cybermen appearing behind the Doctor in the Tardis for a cliffhanger that would lead straight into the Christmas special, 'The Next Doctor'. But Davies started to have doubts about the scene, particularly after being prompted by *Doctor Who Magazine* journalist Benjamin Cook.

The 2010 book *The Writer's Tale: The Final Chapter* reveals how Cook challenged Davies over the episode's original ending. Cook wrote in an email to Davies:

It's too easy. It's not even shocking. It's a bit rubbish, really. It's a watered-down version of the endings to series two and three, even down to the 'What? What?? Whaaat?' gag.

In response, Davis replied:

I think you're right. Right at the back of my mind, I think I'd always thought, right from the moment I typed that last scene, that the runaway bride was brilliant, the Titanic was brilliant, and the Cybermen aren't. They're kind of a poor cousin to those first two cliffhanger surprises.

Davies then came up with an alternative final scene, and during the recording of 'The Next Doctor' in May, Tennant performed extra shots of the Doctor on the Tardis set instead. The original ending was included as an extra on the Fourth Series DVD boxset. The boxset also contains a deleted scene from 'Journey's End' on Bad Wolf Bay, where the Doctor gives Rose a piece of coral from the Tardis, to grow her own ship.

The Specials
'The Next Doctor'
Original UK airdate: 25 December 2008
Cast: David Tennant as The Doctor, David Morrissey as Jackson Lake, Dervla Kirwan as Miss Hartigan, Veilile Tshabalala as Rosita, Ruari Mears as Cybershade, Paul Kasey as Cyberleader, Edmund Kente as Mr Scoones, Michael Bertenshaw as Mr Cole, Jason Morell as Vicar, Neil McDermott as Jed, Ashley Horne as Lad, Tom Langford as Frederic, Jordan Southwell as Urchin, Matthew Allick as Docker and Nicholas Briggs as the voice of the Cybermen
Written by Russell T. Davies
Directed by Andy Goddard
Music by Murray Gold
Produced by Susie Liggat
Filming dates: the main production ran from 7 April to 3 May 2008
Running time: 60 minutes
Original UK viewing figures: 13.1 million

Review
When 'The Next Doctor' was first broadcast, the departure of David Tennant from the role of the Tenth Doctor had already been confirmed, making this episode one gigantic festive tease. After all, the *Doctor Who* production team could not possibly have already filmed an entire Christmas special with a new incarnation without it leaking on the Internet? Could they? Especially with an actor like David Morrissey, who would be top of anyone's wish list as a possible replacement for David Tennant.

As it turns out, Morrissey was not the next Doctor. Instead, he was merely playing Jackson Lake, who thought he might be the Time Lord, which is a shame because in the early scenes, he is full of bravado and daring-do. He really would have made an excellent Doctor. With that out of the way, the production team get to excel themselves by recreating Victorian London in the grounds of Gloucester Cathedral, of all places. The cathedral grounds, which have since been used for an episode starring Jodie Whittaker broadcast in 2020, provide the perfect backdrop, although the cemetery scenes were filmed in dear old Newport.

Dervla Kirwan gets to make the most of Russell T. Davies' daring dialogue and a stunning red dress in the other main role. She really does get to enjoy herself, particularly in the cemetery, when the Cybermen attack for the first time. Never has a femme fatale been so fatal. The showrunner then goes for broke with a giant CyberKing robot marching through the streets of London. It's as daft a concept as they come, mixing Charles Dickens and steampunk, although the robot itself looks quite impressive. Quite why nobody ever remembers this annual tradition of aliens taking over the capital remains a mystery. Like all the other Christmas specials, 'The Next Doctor' is best enjoyed through a haze of sherry trifle and mince pies. Sometimes, it's best not to overthink such things.

The story

The Tardis lands on the streets of London. It is Christmas Eve in 1851, and everyone is full of festive cheer, but as the Doctor walks around he hears a young woman called Rosita calling for him. He runs to help but finds another man, also calling himself the Doctor, who has a sonic screwdriver and a Tardis of his own. A creature emerges with a Cyberman's face called a Cybershade. The 'next' Doctor tries to lasso the creature but is instead dragged up a large wall. The Tenth Doctor grabs the rope and tries to help and gets dragged along too.

The 'next' Doctor admits large parts of his memory are missing. The earliest thing he remembers is being attacked by the Cybermen, who have landed in Victorian London. The two Doctors enter the home of the late Reverend Audrey Fairchild, where they find some infostamps, which are used by the Cybermen to store vital information. Meanwhile, a woman called Miss Mercy Hartigan attends the funeral of Reverend Fairchild in a striking red dress. She summons an army of Cybermen, who appear from the fog and attack the other mourners. They spare only four men, who all run workhouses.

The Tenth Doctor returns with the 'next' Doctor to his Tardis, which is a giant hot-air balloon and stands for 'Tethered Aerial Release Developed In-Style'.

Meanwhile, the four workhouse masters are put under Miss Hartigan's direct control by the Cybermen. The Tenth Doctor realises the other Doctor is, in fact, Jackson Lake, who has been missing for some time. The Time Lord deduces that Jackson was attacked by the Cybermen and used an infostamp containing information on the Doctor to fight them off. Somehow, the information entered his mind and led him to believe he was the Doctor.

The possessed workhouse masters start leading their children through the streets of London. Miss Hartigan kills the masters and puts the children to work in an underground base, generating electricity for a giant steampunk robot, the CyberKing.

The Cybermen inform Miss Hartigan that she is also to be converted and she is placed on a throne, which is situated in the chest of the CyberKing. The Doctor and Jackson discover the base. As they rescue the children, Jackson spots a little boy, who he realises is his son. The Doctor rescues the boy and reunites father and son. But the CyberKing is now towering above the streets of London. The Doctor takes Jackson's hot-air balloon and starts firing info stamps at Miss Hartigan.

As the CyberKing starts to topple, the Doctor uses a Dimension Vault to make it vanish. With the Cybermen defeated, the Doctor accepts Jackson's invitation to Christmas dinner.

Trivia and facts

Russell T. Davies' original idea for the 2008 Christmas special involved JK Rowling being attacked by a time creature and transported back to a Victorian world where the Doctor would have to battle witches and wizards to reach her. But the idea was shelved, as it seemed unlikely that the Harry Potter author would agree to appear as herself. Another idea involved the father of a family, who had left his wife and children in a hotel room at Christmas and ventured out to fetch some ice, only to return to the room and find it empty. The other Doctor's companion is named Rosita, which is a partial combination of Rose and Martha.

Davies had considered using the title 'Court of the Cyber King', before opting for 'The Next Doctor'. At this point, it was well established that David Tennant would be moving on from the role, which helped increased interest in the story.

Because of licensing concerns, it was not clear if a shot of Paul McGann's Eighth Doctor from the 1996 Doctor Who TV Movie would be available, so a shot of the actor as Liam Phelan in the 1995 BBC drama The Hanging Gale was held in reserve, just in case.

St. Woolios Cemetery, on Bassaleg Road in Newport, was covered in fake snow for the graveyard scenes. The stables and courtyard at Tredegar House were dressed up as ironmongers. Tennant celebrated his 37th birthday while filming more scenes for 'The Next Doctor' at Hensol Castle in the Vale of Glamorgan on 18 April 2008. The crew then moved to the streets around Gloucester Cathedral, which doubled as a Victorian market, complete with more fake snow. Some of the Cyber HQ scenes were filmed on the Torchwood Hub set at Upper Boat Studios, which had been redressed for the festive special. The last day of filming was 3 May 2008 with Dervla Kirwan shooting the remaining CyberKing throne sequences. On the same day, David Tennant was on the Tardis set, recording, instead, for the 2008 Doctor Who at the Proms event, which was held at the Royal Albert Hall in London later that summer, on 27 July 2008.

'Planet of the Dead'

Original UK airdate: 11 April 2009
Cast: David Tennant as The Doctor, Michelle Ryan as Christina, Lee Evans as Malcolm, Noma Dumezweni as Capt. Magambo, Adam James as DI McMillan, Glenn Doherty as Sgt. Dennison, Victoria Alcock as Angela, David Ames as Nathan, Eilen Thomas as Carmen, Reginald Tsiboe as Lou, Daniel Kaluuya as Barclay, Keith Parry as the Bus Driver, James Layton as Sgt. Ian Jenner, Paul Kasey as Sorvin and Ruari Mears as Praygat
Written by Russell T. Davies and Gareth Roberts
Directed by James Strong
Music by Murray Gold
Produced by Tracie Simpson
Filming dates: the main production ran from 19 January to 18 February 2009
Running time: 58 minutes
Original UK viewing figures: 9.7 million

Review

For all the hype at the time when it was originally broadcast, 'Planet of the Dead' must rank as one of the silliest *Doctor Who* adventures of all time. Re-watching it all these years later, there is a nagging feeling the planning meeting started and finished with the words 'big red bus in a desert'. Now admittedly, a double-decker in the middle of a barren planet is a brilliant image, but an hour-long special might need a bit more to keep the viewers interested.

'Planet of the Dead' does start off in style with a brilliantly filmed heist. Michelle Ryan quickly establishes herself as Lady Christina, and yes, the desert does look impressive, particularly as this was the first episode of Doctor Who to be shot in high definition. But the plot itself rapidly runs out of steam. The Doctor and his fellow travellers find themselves on an alien planet. They need a gizmo to get the bus going again. They find said gizmo and they go home, narrowly avoiding a swarm of nasty aliens on the way. Oh, and the bus flies at the end, because who doesn't love a flying bus?

It's all quite daft, but at least it has the decency not to take itself too seriously. The Tritovore aliens were a blatant homage to the bug-eyed monsters of yesteryear. Although they look good, they play a fairly inconsequential role. At least 'Planet of the Dead' has Lee Evans shamelessly mugging as UNIT scientist Malcolm - he really should have his own Big Finish spin-off audio adventure and Lady Christina already does. Carmen's prophecy at the end is a sign that things are about to get very dark for the Tenth Doctor, which they do, but 'Planet of the Dead' is the Time Lord's (and the viewers too, for that matter) last chance for a bit of fun.

The story

A glamorous cat burglar called Lady Christina de Souza stages a daring robbery at the International Gallery, where she steals a valuable golden goblet. She tries to make her escape, but the police are in hot pursuit, so she decides to jump on a passing double-decker bus. The Doctor also gets on the bus and sits down next to Lady Christina and wishes her a happy Easter.

The bus is spotted by the police, who gave chase. When the bus enters a long, underground tunnel, the police order the other end to be closed. Then as the bus drives through the tunnel, it enters a wormhole and is suddenly transported to a desolate desert planet. As the passengers examine the damage to the bus, the driver decides to walk back through the wormhole, which kills him. One of the passengers, Carmen, becomes increasingly agitated. She can hear the voices of the dead all around her.

A squad of UNIT soldiers set up base at the end of the tunnel, which is led by Captain Erisa Magambo and helped by a scientific adviser, Malcolm Taylor, who is a big fan of the Doctor. The Doctor and Lady Christina go exploring and are captured by an insectoid alien, called a Tritovore. It takes them to its crashed spaceship. The Doctor scans the approaching sandstorm and discovers it is a swarm of flying parasites.

They created the wormhole and want to use it to travel to Earth, which they will strip bare. Lady Christina uses her cat burglar skills to get a power crystal from the heart of the ship, which the Doctor uses to make the bus fly back through the wormhole. Three parasites manage to get through before Malcolm manages it to close the wormhole. Fortunately, the UNIT soldiers are able to shoot the parasites down. The police arrest Lady Christina, but she escapes and flies off in the bus. As the Doctor returns to the Tardis, Carmen gives him a chilling premonition. The Time Lord's song is ending and that 'he will knock four times'.

Trivia and facts
Russell T. Davies originally envisaged the Easter 2009 special being an out-and-out space opera, in the style of *Star Wars*, with the Tardis materialising in the middle of a large intergalactic battle. Writer Gareth Roberts was then approached to work with Davies on the episode. The showrunner was quite taken with the image of a tube train on a desert planet, which featured in Roberts' 1993 Virgin Doctor Who novel *The Highest Science*. Early drafts also featured a new sidekick, called Rebecca, who was working as a tour guide on an open-topped bus. But as the writing process continued, this character was replaced with a top-class jewel thief, initially called Hermione.

The production team bought two near-identical 1980 Bristol BLMC VR buses for the story. One was used on location in Cardiff and the studio, while the other travelled to Dubai for the desert sequences. The Dubai bus left Cardiff in early December 2008 and was driven to the London Thamesport Container Terminal, where it was lifted onto an open pallet and lashed down to the ship's deck for the journey to Dubai. The bus arrived safe and sound at the container dock in Jebel Ali, which is southwest of Dubai, but on 5 January 2009 there was an accident at the port which caused substantial damage to the bus. After briefly considering getting a replacement bus, Davies decided to change the script and put in some lines about the vehicle being damaged as it travelled through the wormhole.

The opening museum heist was filmed at the atrium of the Welsh National Museum in Cardiff, with Michelle Ryan performing many of her own stunts. The Queen's Gate Tunnel on the A4232 in Butedown, which was closed down for four nights to allow maintenance, was used to record all the tunnel sequences. The cast and crew departed for Dubai on 10 February 2009, where they stayed at the Holiday Arabian Resort in Hatta. The first day of filming (12 February) was disrupted by one of the worst sandstorms in recent months. Fortunately, the following day the weather improved and filming resumed.

'The Waters of Mars'
Original UK airdate: 15 November 2009
Cast: David Tennant as The Doctor, Lindsay Duncan as Adelaide Brooke, Peter O'Brien as Ed Gold, Aleksandar Mikic as Yuri Kerenski, Gemma Chan as Mia Bennett, Sharon Duncan-Brewster as Maggie Cain, Chook Sibtain as Tarak Ital, Alan Ruscoe as Andy Stone, Cosima Shaw as Steffi Ehrlich, Michael Goldsmith as Roman Groom, Lily Bevan as Emily, Max Bollinger as Mikhail, Charlie De'Ath as Adelaide's Father, Rachel Fewell as Young Adelaide, Anouska Strahnz as Ulrika Ehrlich, Zofia

Strahnz as Lisette Ehrlich and Paul Kasey at Ood Sigma
Written by Russell T. Davies and Phil Ford
Directed by Graeme Harper
Music by Murray Gold
Produced by Nikki Wilson
Filming dates: the main production ran from 23 February to 20 March 2009, with an additional filming day on 15 May
Running time: 62 minutes
Original UK viewing figures: 10.3 million

Review

As previously mentioned elsewhere in this book, the 'base under siege' format is fertile ground for *Doctor Who* and 'The Waters of Mars' is no exception. Except this time, it's dark. Really dark. It's been said that Doctor Who cannot do Aliens-style terror, but this is close.

Russell T. Davies and co-writer Phil Ford go all out with some of the most horrific images ever seen on the show. The water monsters are genuinely terrifying. If there is one Doctor Who story that will give you nightmares, then it might be this one, even if the water monsters run down corridors like your granny. Just don't mention the Gadget robot, which is very, very annoying. Even the Doctor cannot stand him, which should tell you something.

'The Waters of Mars' is a highly polished rollercoaster with the sense of dread and doom slowly building over the course of the first act. As a viewer, you know everything is about to go wrong, and it does. And just this once, the Doctor is powerless to help. The point about the Time Lord not being able to change fixed points in history has been laboured again and again, but this time it becomes a vital part of the plot.

We also get to see the Tenth Doctor go from happy, go-lucky traveller to frustrated, and eventually, to an out-of-control Time Lord. His descent into anger and breaking the laws of time reminds you just how fine an actor David Tennant is. Younger viewers will find it all a little too scary and the final scenes on Earth are some of the darkest ever filmed on the series with a character taking their own life. The final days of the Tenth Doctor were never going to be fun and games, but a decade on, 'The Waters of Mars' still retains the power to shock.

The story

The Tardis takes the Doctor to Mars, where he joins a group of space explorers on Bowie Base One. The crew include Captain Adelaide Brooke, a robot called Gadget and several other crew members. Elsewhere, another crew member, Andy Stone, washes some carrots grown in the base's bio-dome and washes them in water. He bites one of the carrots and immediately starts to convulse. Moments later, the skin on his face is cracked and water is dribbling from his mouth.

While talking to Captain Brooke, the Doctor realises it is 21 November 2059, which is a fixed date in history. It is the day the base is destroyed in a nuclear blast, killing all the crew, including Captain Brooke. The Time Lord says he must leave, but before he can, a strange noise is heard through the base's speakers, coming from the bio-dome. Captain Brooke insists the Doctor come with her to investigate what is going on. They find another crew member, Maggie Cain, lying unconscious with a head wound. She is taken to sickbay and quarantined, but the Doctor, Captain Brooke and crew member Tarak continue into the bio-dome.

In the dome, Andy attacks Tarak Ital and infects him with water shooting out of his hands. In the sickbay, Maggie starts to convulse and becomes infected too. The Doctor and Captain Brooke manage to escape from the bio-dome, with the possessed Andy and Tarak in hot pursuit. She orders the base to be evacuated, but the Doctor warns her that she risks taking the infection back to Earth.

The Doctor walks away from the base. The deputy base commander, Ed Gold, starts preparing the base's rocket for evacuation, but more crew members become infected. He activates the rocket's self-destruction system and sacrifices himself.

As the rocket explodes, the Doctor realises there is nothing to stop him changing the course of history, and so he returns, seals the dome and rescues the remaining crew members, Captain Brooke, Mia Bennett and Yuri Kerenski.

He takes them back on the Tardis to Earth. Mia and Yuri run off, but Captain Brooke becomes appalled the Doctor says he has the power to change history. He is the 'Time Lord victorious' and there's nobody who can stop him. She walks into her home and takes her own life. The Doctor is visibly shocked as he realises that he has gone too far, and history has not changed after all. Then Ood Sigma appears in the street but says nothing. The Doctor walks back into the Tardis and hears the cloister bell ring. Refusing to accept his fate, he departs in the Tardis once again.

Trivia and facts

When developing ideas for the next 2009 special, Russell T. Davies originally returned to the idea of a family staying in a London hotel at Christmas (see 'The Next Doctor'). The story would have involved a grandmother, who had wished all her relatives would disappear. When she got up to get some ice, she found the hotel was deserted and on returning to the family room, she discovered they too had vanished.

The old lady then staggered outside the hotel, only to find the streets of London completely empty, save for a police box. She then knocked on the door and met the Doctor. But then Davies started to become concerned about the cost of recreating empty streets and a hotel within the show's budget.

Another idea was to link the previous special with this story by having it end with the Doctor hearing a knock at the Tardis door, and being confronted by an old woman – possibly played by Dame Helen Mirren - who needed his help.

Davies gave co-writer Phil Ford the idea of 'Christmas on Mars', which would be set on a Martian base in the near future, but he preferred the original hotel storyline.

As Ford and Davies worked on possible story ideas, NASA announced that it had discovered evidence of water on Mars, which prompted a change in direction for the script. At one point, the worldwide credit crunch meant that there were questions over whether this special would go ahead. BBC Worldwide, which is the Corporation's commercial arm, was struggling following the collapse of Woolworths. The much-missed high street chain and BBC Worldwide had a joint interest in the DVD company 2|entertain and money from sales of the show to Japan had vanished. However, the finances were secured and the production was allowed to go ahead.

The relationship between Yuri and Mia was edited out during post-production because Julie Gardner wanted the action to move faster. The Great Glasshouse at the National Botanic Garden of Wales in Llanarthne, Carmarthenshire was used to film the space station's biodome scenes. Victoria Place in Newport was covered with fake snow for the story's dramatic conclusion. One shot of the Doctor by the Tardis in Victoria Place was later reshot on the Brandon Estate in South London, during the filming of 'The End of Time'.

'The End of Time (Parts One and Two)'

Original UK airdate: 25 December 2009 and 1 January 2010
Cast: David Tennant as The Doctor, John Simm as The Master, Bernard Cribbins as Wilfred Mott, Timothy Dalton as The Narrator/Lord President, Catherine Tate as Donna Noble, Jacqueline King as Sylvia Noble, Billie Piper as Rose Tyler, Camille Coduri as Jackie Tyler, John Barrowman as Captain Jack Harkness, Freema Agyeman as Martha Smith-Jones, Noel Clarke as Mickey Smith, Elisabeth Sladen as Sarah Jane Smith, Jessica Hynes as Verity Newman, Claire Bloom as The Woman, June Whitfield as Minnie Hooper, Thomas Knight as Luke Smith, Russell Tovey as Midshipman Frame, David Harewood as Joshua Naismith, Tracey Ifeachor as Abigail Naismith, Sinead Keenan as Addams, Lawry Lewin as Rossiter, Joe Dixon as The Chancellor, Julie Legrand as The Partisan, Brid Brennan as The Visionary, Alexandra Moen as Lucy Saxon, Karl Collins as Shaun Temple, Krystal Archer as Nerys, Silas Carson as the voice of Ood Sigma, Brian Cox as the voice of Elder Ood, Nicholas Briggs as the voice of the Judoon, Dan Starkey as Sontaran and introducing Matt Smith as The Doctor
Written by Russell T. Davies
Directed by Euros Lyn
Music by Murray Gold
Produced by Tracie Simpson
Filming dates: the main production ran from 21 March to 22 May March 2009, with an additional filming day on 3 June
Running time: 59/72 minutes
Original UK viewing figures: 12/12.2 million

Review

Regeneration stories can be problematic at times because, let's face it, we all know how they are going to end for the Doctor and that's not very well. Like the Third Doctor's swansong 'Planet of the Spiders' and the Fourth Doctor's parting shot 'Logopolis', 'The End of Time' is all about the end of an era, with the central character about to be killed off before our very eyes. While 'The End of Time' certainly feels like a turning point in the show's history, it is overblown and overlong. Inside the combined running time of more than two hours and 15 minutes, there's a slimmer and more powerful version just waiting to be found.

Part of the problem is that, with the exception of the Master and the Time Lords returning, not a lot happens in the first half. Claire Bloom shows up as The Woman and gets to be all mysterious, but then she vanishes again. There's also a terrific scene where the Master gets to shoot lightning bolts at the Doctor, and that's about it. The plot only kicks into gear in the second half with John Simm delivering a more restrained and improved version of the Master.

Despite the running time, the script does keep you guessing about how the Tenth Doctor is going to die. The revelation that it is Wilfred Mott who will knock four times is heart-breaking for the viewers and the Doctor alike. Watching the Doctor rail against his fate proves just how much the world will miss this character. But the power of that scene is undone by the lengthy coda at the end, which rivals the movie adaptation of Lord of the Rings for stringing it - well and truly - out. Getting the Doctor to say goodbye to one companion is fair enough, but all of them? Even the granddaughter of nurse Joan ('Human Nature/Family of Blood') Redfern? You can't blame Russell T. Davies for wanting to tie up all the loose ends, but even so. The final scenes between the Tenth Doctor and Rose do not disappoint and as the Time Lord staggers back to the Tardis, there is not a dry eye in the house. The Tenth Doctor gets the send-off he deserves, even if it takes a little time to get there. His song might have finished, but the story never ends.

The story

While out Christmas shopping one night, Wilfred Mott visits a church, where he sees a Tardis in the stained window. A woman in white appears next to him and says it is a legend that involves a 'sainted physician' who disappeared but might be returning. In another part of the galaxy, the Doctor meets the Ood elders. As the Doctor communes with the creatures, he sees pictures of the Master, Wilf and the Master's wife, Lucy Saxon.

Back on Earth, Lucy Saxon is escorted from her prison cell to meet the new governor, who is a disciple of the Master. The governor uses a ring stolen from the Master's funeral pyre and Lucy's biometrical signature to start a ceremony to bring the renegade back to life. As the Master returns, Lucy throws a vial into the fire, which causes him and the prison to explode.

A wealthy businessman, Joshua Naismith examines the footage of the explosion and spots someone fleeing from the wreckage. Meanwhile, Wilf has enlisted the help of his retired friends in a bid to locate the Doctor. The Doctor eventually finds the Master, who is mentally unbalanced and hiding in wasteland. But as the Doctor approaches his old enemy, a helicopter appears overhead and the Master is kidnapped by armed guards, who take the Master to Naismith's mansion. The businessman shows the Master a device found in a crashed spaceship, called the Immortality Gate. The device is currently inoperable, but Naismith wants to get it running again, so his daughter Abigail can live forever.

The Tardis lands in the mansion stables and the Doctor and Wilf head inside. They discover two scientists – Addams and Rossiter – are Vinvocci aliens in disguise. They explain the gate is a device to transmit medical templates across entire planets at a time.

The Doctor races to the Gate room, but it is too late. The Master uses the Gate to transmit his DNA to every human being on Earth. Suddenly everyone is the Master, apart from Wilf who is in a radiation shield booth and Donna Noble, who is part Time Lord. Back on Gallifrey, as the Time War enters its final hours, Lord President Rassilon is busy planning the return of the Time Lords. Rassilon is told of a prophecy, that talks of two children of Gallifrey surviving the Time War and locked in a final confrontation on Earth. He believes the prophecy refers to the Doctor and the Master.

Back on Earth, the Master is holding the Doctor and Wilf captive and gloating at his success. They manage to escape with the Vinvocci aliens and teleport back to their spaceship, which is in orbit above the planet. On Gallifrey, Rassilon decides to implant a drumbeat inside the Master's head as a young boy. Back in the present day, the Master focuses on that drumbeat, creating a link with Gallifrey.

But the signal is not strong enough, so Rassilon sends a Whitepoint Star jewel to Earth to make physical contact. The Doctor sees the Whitepoint Star fly into the Earth's atmosphere and realises what is happening. He flies the Vinvocci spaceship back to the Naismith mansion.

The Master sets the nuclear bolt source to maximum in the gate room and uses the Whitepoint Star to bring Gallifrey back from the Time War. After dodging countless missiles, the Doctor jumps from the ship and crash lands in the Gate Room, but it is too late. Rassilon and a group of Time Lords are standing there in front of him. The Lord President snaps his fingers, and everyone on Earth is returned to normal. He then says he wants to bring about the end of time itself. Realising that the Time Lords were responsible for the drumbeat inside his head, the Master launches himself at them, firing bolts from his hands. The Time Lords and Gallifrey vanish back into the Time War.

The Doctor lies on the floor of the Gate Room, thinking he has been saved. Then he hears the sound of Wilf knocking four times on the glass of the radiation shield booth. His heart breaks as he realises that the prophecy about 'he will knock four times' was never about the Master. It was about Wilf. And now the nuclear bolt will vent into Wilf's booth and kill the old man. The Doctor's only option is to go into the other booth and let the radiation flood that booth instead. The radiation dose is lethal, and the Doctor collapses to the floor. A few moments later, he wakes up and leaves the booth. The regeneration process has started.

The Doctor drops Wilf off at this home and says he is off to get 'my reward'. He saves Martha and Mickey Smith from a Sontaran. Then he turns up at Donna Noble's wedding, where he gives Wilf a winning lottery ticket. Finally, he returns to the Powell Estate in 2005, where he wishes Rose Tyler a happy new year.

As the regeneration process starts to take over, the Doctor starts to stumble towards the Tardis, and Ood Sigma appears. 'This song is ending, but the story never ends,' says Ood Sigma as the Tenth Doctor takes his final steps into the Tardis. 'I don't want to go,' cries out the Doctor as his body explodes with regeneration energy. Every single cell starts to change. A new incarnation of the Doctor now stands in his place. The era of the Eleventh Doctor has begun and he must act fast as the Tardis is crashing. Geronimo!

Trivia and facts

Russell T. Davies came up with the Tenth Doctor's final words 'I don't want to go' while he was writing 'Partners in Crime', but he kept them to himself. The showrunner also told Catherine Tate that he wanted Donna Noble to return for the Tenth Doctor's finale at the 2008 series wrap party and made her promise she would come back.

His initial idea for the finale involved the Tardis landing on a small spaceship, which would be manned by a family. When the ship's engine threatened to leak, the Doctor would sacrifice his own life, by entering the engine room and taking a fatal dose of radiation, instead of the family's father. Concerned that this might be seen as an anti-climax, he then returned to the idea of a rematch between the Doctor and the Master.

Davies worked closely with the incoming showrunner Steven Moffat, who wrote the final scene with Matt Smith as the Eleventh Doctor. Moffat's only stipulation was that the Tenth Doctor wore a tie for his regeneration. The scene in Part Two, where the Tenth Doctor is wheeled away, having been strapped to a chair, created a few challenges as Tennant had undergone a back operation in December 2008. A life-size dummy, complete with Tennant's face, was used for some of those scenes.

The character referred to as 'The Woman' has been the subject of much debate over the years.

In The Writer's Tale, Davies says he told actress Claire Bloom that she is:

Meant to be the Doctor's mother. It could only be his mother, really. If I can't imagine a world in which our mothers are there, at the end of our lives, in our time of need, to help us, then what's the point?

To accommodate Jessica Hynes, a one-off filming day was held on 21 March 2009, with the Doctor Who crew at the Cardiff University Branch of Blackwell's Bookshop for the scene where Verity Newman signs a copy of her book for the Doctor.

The main production started on 30 March at Tredegar House in Newport, which doubled for the Naismith's mansion. The scene where the now-married Martha and Mickey Smith evade the Sontarans was filmed at Corus Strip Products' Llanwern Works in Newport. St Mary's Church in Marshfield, near Newport, was the location for Donna Noble's wedding. As the churchyard scenes were being recorded, an effects team set up a crater in the field next to the church for a scene featuring John Simm later that night. The Wookie Hole caves near Wells in Somerset were transformed into an ice cave for the Ood, while the scene where Wilf meets 'the Woman' inside the church was filmed at St. Augustine's Church in Penarth.

The regeneration scene was filmed at Upper Boat Studios on 11 May 2009. Four different versions of the Doctor's final line were filmed, with the Time Lord increasingly distressed in each take. The third, more stoical take was eventually used, as it was felt the Doctor should not lose his bravery in his final moment.

After Tennant's shots were completed, he left the set along with Julie Gardner and Russell T. Davies, and incoming Doctor Matt Smith, showrunner Steven Moffat and executive producer Piers Wenger took charge of the Eleventh Doctor's debut scene.

Tennant's last day filming for the series was 20 May 2009, which concluded at 6.49 pm with a piece of wirework. Once that was completed, he returned to his trailer but was later called back for a 'lighting reference'.When he returned to the set, an air cannon filled with pink confetti was fired and first assistant director, Peter Bennett announced:

That's a golden wrap on the Tenth Doctor, Mr David Tennant!

Later appearances

Introduction

Being such an ardent fan himself, many people considered it would be a question of when, not if, David Tennant would return to the role of The Doctor. Even so, the speed of his return surprised many. His last day filming on 'The End of Time' on *Doctor Who* was 20 May 2009. But by 25 May, he was back filming as the Tenth Doctor, but this time as a guest star on the BBC spin-off show *The Sarah Jane Adventures*. But in true timey-wimey fashion, 'The Wedding of Sarah Jane Smith' was broadcast in October 2009, before 'The End of Time' and the official end of the Tenth Doctor's era.

In the run-up to the show's 50th anniversary in 2013, there was renewed hope that Tennant would team up with his successor, Matt Smith and other Doctors for a feature-length special. On 30 March 2013 came the news that all Doctor Who fans were hoping for, with the confirmation that both Tennant and Billie Piper would be joining an all-star cast for the anniversary special to be broadcast in November 2013.

Tennant said in an interview issued by the BBC Press Office for the 50th anniversary:

> It's very exciting to be around for the big celebration episode. I think since I left, the expectation had been that I'd end up in this special because there is a precedent for old Doctors coming back for a visit around the anniversary time. I was thrilled because it's a huge thing for *Doctor Who* and it's a huge thing for television in general. So, few shows run beyond a few series and 50 years' worth is quite a legacy, so I'm very honoured to be part of that.

On the 26 October 2015, it was announced that Tennant would be reprising the role of the Tenth Doctor on audio for Big Finish Production, alongside his co-star, Catherine Tate. The first volume of *Doctor Who: The Tenth Doctor Adventures* was released by Big Finish in May 2016 and comprised three full-cast audio adventures –'Technophobia' by Matt Fitton, 'Time Reaver' by Jenny T.Colgan and 'Death and the Queen' by James Goss. Said Big Finish's executive producer Jason Haigh-Ellery, when the news first broke of his return in 2015:

> I still remember the sense of joy I had when I heard that David had been asked to play the Doctor. We were all so pleased for him — as we knew how much Doctor Who meant to him. And now David comes full circle, back doing Doctor Who with Big Finish — except that this time he's playing the Doctor! It's the same but different — it's wonderful to have him back!

In November 2017, Big Finish released the second volume of *Doctor Who: The Tenth Doctor Adventures*, which saw Tennant reunite with Billie Piper as

Rose Tyler for three new adventures –'Infamy of the Zaross' by John Dorney, 'The Sword of the Chevalier' by Guy Adams and 'Cold Vengeance' by Matt Fitton. And in May 2019, Big Finish released the third instalment of *The Tenth Doctor Adventures* with Tennant and Tate back in the driving seat. The three adventures in Volume 3 are 'No Place' by James Goss, 'One Mile Down' by Jenny T. Colgan and 'The Creeping Death' by Roy Gill.' Commented Big Finish's executive producer Nicholas Briggs in 2015:

> I've enjoyed working with all the Doctors on TV, but David is the only one
> I'd known before he became the Doctor. I'd worked with him on our *Dalek Empire* series for Big Finish and had such fun. So along with the excitement of directing new Tenth Doctor adventures, I'm so happy to be working with an old chum again'

Big Finish are due to release a spin-off audio series in May 2020 starring Catherine Tate entitled *Donna Noble – Kidnapped!* which will also feature a guest appearance by Tennant as The Doctor. As for future appearances, to quote the Curator himself, who knows, who knows, eh?

'The Wedding of Sarah Jane Smith (Parts One and Two)'

Original UK airdate: 29/30 October 2009
Cast: Elisabeth Sladen as Sarah Jane Smith, Tommy Knight as Luke Smith, Daniel Anthony as Clyde Langer, Anjli Mohindra as Rani Chandra, David Tennant as The Doctor, Nigel Havers as Peter Dalton, Mina Anwar as Gita, Ace Bhatti as Haresh, Alexander Armstrong as the voice of Mr Smith, John Leeson as the voice of K-9, Parl Marc Davis at the Trickster and Zienia Merton as the Registrar
Written by Gareth Roberts
Directed by Joss Agnew
Music by Murray Gold, Sam Watts and Dan Watts
Produced by Nikki Wilson/Phil Ford
Filming dates: the main production ran from 15 May to 2 June 2009
Running time: 27/28minutes
Original UK viewing figures: 1.5/1.4 million

Review

'The Wedding of Sarah Jane Smith' is a victory lap for the Tenth Doctor, even though he only appears in the last 30 seconds of the first episode. But despite this minor quibble, the two-parter is a joy and deserves its place in the *Doctor Who* canon. The Sarah Jane Adventures were designed for a much younger audience, and fresh from filming 'The End of Time', Tennant seems to relish the chance to play a slightly lighter version of the Doctor and share centre stage with the series regulars. However, older viewers will find the scenes between Sarah Jane and Peter particularly moving, thanks to the richness of Gareth Robert's script. Nigel Havers might be rehashing his dashing gent for

111

the millionth time running, but his final moments pack an emotional punch, proving the old charmer still has it. The final parting scene between Sarah Jane and the Doctor won't leave a dry eye in the house and quite right too.

The story

Luke, Rani and Clyde become suspicious when Sarah Jane Smith starts acting in an unusual and furtive manner. They decide to investigate but are shocked to find Sarah Jane on a dinner date with a handsome man, called Peter Dalton. The romance quickly blooms and Peter proposes to Sarah Jane. Her engagement seems to have a strange effect on the investigate journalist, who announces they will be married the following week and she is shutting down the Mr Smith supercomputer in the attic. Rani and Clyde are suspicious and visit Peter's home, but they find his house is empty. It is soon the day of the wedding, and the guests gather in a country hotel. The Registrar begins the ceremony, but before they can be declared man and wife, the Tenth Doctor rushes in and demands that the wedding be stopped. The Trickster than appears and kidnaps bride and groom.

Most of the guests then also vanish, leaving just the Doctor, Luke, Rani and Clyde, along with K-9, to figure out what just happened. The Doctor realises they are all trapped in a split second of time. In the other time zone, Peter tells Sarah Jane he was visited by an angel (The Trickster) after he fell down the stairs at home, offering his life and a love he never had. The Trickster warns Sarah Jane and Peter will remain trapped forever if she does not agree to be under his power. The Doctor decides to use the artron energy, which powers the Tardis to fight the Trickster. As Clyde tries to enter the Tardis, the doors slam shut and he is infused with artron energy.

Newly-energised, Clyde decides to fight the Trickster and temporarily disable the creature. Sarah Jane realises the only way to defeat the Trickster is for Peter to reject the alien's original agreement, after the accident at home. Peter sacrifices himself to save Sarah Jane and defeat the Trickster, restoring everyone to their current time zones.

Trivia and facts

'The Wedding of Sarah Jane' was also due to have featured the return of another Doctor Who character, Sir Alistair Lethbridge-Stewart, who featured in early drafts of the script. Unfortunately, as filming drew near, the actor who played the legendary Brigadier, Nicholas Courtney had to pull out because of ill health.

The BBC press office announced on 26 May 2009 that Tennant was to appear in The Sarah Jane Adventures. Showrunner Russell T. Davies, referring to the broadcast of the next special 'The Waters of Mars', said:

Viewers thought they may have to wait until November for the next full episode of Doctor Who, but this is an extra special treat. And it's not just a cameo from David – this is a full-on appearance for the Doctor as he and Sarah Jane face their biggest threat ever.

During the week of filming, Tennant also managed to travel up to London to record the Christmas edition of the panel game *QI*, before returning the next day. His last day of filming was 29 May 2009. The Tenth Doctor's last line in front of the camera was

You two – with me! Spit spot!

'The Day of the Doctor '
Original UK airdate: 23 November 2013
Cast: Matt Smith as The Doctor, David Tennant as The Doctor, Jenna Coleman as Clare, Billie Piper as Rose, John Hurt as The Doctor, Tristan Beint as Tom, Jemma Redgrave as Kate Stewart, Ingrid Oliver as Osgood, Chris Finch as Time Lord Soldier, Peter De Jersey as Androgar, Ken Bones as The General, Philip Buck as Arcadia Father, Sophie Morgan-Price as Time Lord, Joanna Page as Elizabeth I, Orlando James as Lord Bentham, Jonjo O'Neill as McGillop, Tom Keller as Atkins, Aidan Cook as a Zygon, Paul Kasey as a Zygon, Nicholas Briggs as the voice of the Daleks and the Zygons, Barnaby Edwards as Dalek 1, Nicholas Pegg as Dalek 2, John Guilor as Voice Over Artist, Tom Baker as the Curator, with appearances by William Hartnell, Patrick Troughton, Jon Pertwee, Tom Baker, Peter Davison, Colin Baker, Sylvester McCoy, Paul McGann and Christopher Eccleston as The Doctor
Written by Steven Moffat
Directed by Nick Huran
Music by Murray Gold
Produced by Marcus Wilson
Filming dates: the main production ran from 28 March to 4 May 2013, with an additional day of filming on 3 October
Running time: 76 minutes
Original UK viewing figures: 12.8 million

Review
Steven Moffat's tenure as *Doctor Who* showrunner was not without its critics, who frequently complained that the plots became too complicated and too adult in tone. With problems behind the scenes, not least Christopher Eccleston backing out and the fans high expectations for a 50th anniversary special, 'The Day of the Doctor' could have been an unmitigated mess, but Moffat snatched victory from the jaws of defeat, giving us one of the finest *Doctor Who* stories of all time. David Tennant slips effortlessly back into the role that made him a household name and John Hurt turns in a memorable performance as the hitherto unknown War Doctor. The Zygon plot gets short shrift in the final act, but the prospect of every incarnation of the Doctor, however briefly on screen, even the as-yet-unseen Thirteenth Doctor, saving

the universe, was every fan's dream come true. Moffat pulls off a seemingly impossible feat by sorting out all the loose ends of the Time War and he even managed to give the long-running show another direction to travel in. The cameo appearance by the oldest surviving actor to have played the Time Lord, Tom Baker, is the icing on the birthday cake. 'The Day of the Doctor' was not just Steven Moffat's finest hour, it was a fitting tribute to 50 years of adventures in time and space.

The story

The Eleventh Doctor and Clara are summoned to the National Gallery in London by UNIT, where they find a painting which once belonged to Queen Elizabeth I, called 'Gallifrey Falls'. Meanwhile, the War Doctor is fighting in the last days of the Time War on Gallifrey. He steals a weapon called 'The Moment' from the Time Lords and takes it to an isolated barn. A young woman, who looks like Rose Tyler, appears and reveals she is the Moment's interface. She knows he plans to use it to end the Time War by destroying Gallifrey and the Daleks in one go. Back in 1562, the Tenth Doctor proposes to Elizabeth I, thinking she is a shape-shifting Zygon. When it transpires that it is actually her horse that is the Zygon, he gives chase into the woods, but then a time fissure opens up and a fez hat falls through it.

In the modern-day, the Eleventh Doctor acquires a fez as he walks into another part of the National Gallery. UNIT's Kate Stewart shows him another set of paintings, which have all been smashed from the inside. Then a time fissure opens up. The Eleventh Doctor throws his fez into it, before jumping through it himself.

The Eleventh Doctor finds himself in 1562 and standing in front of the Tenth Doctor. They are soon joined by the War Doctor, who is looking for his other incarnations.

The three Doctors are taken prisoner and taken to the Tower of London. In the modern day, Kate takes Clara to the Black Archive under the Tower of London, where UNIT has Captain Jack Harkness's vortex manipulator. After it is revealed that Kate is a Zygon, Clara uses to the manipulator to go back to 1562, where she finds all the Doctors squabbling in a cell.

The Eleventh Doctor arranges for the Gallifrey Falls painting to be put in the Black Archive, with all the Doctors inside it. They then emerge and force the human Kate and the Zygon Kate to cooperate.

The Three Doctors then return to the barn on Gallifrey, where the Eleventh Doctor says he has an idea. He suggests they put his homeworld in a pocket universe, so the Daleks will be destroyed by their own crossfire. All thirteen incarnations of the Doctor are summoned and Gallifrey is saved.

Afterwards, the Eleventh Doctor meets a familiar-looking curator at the National Gallery, who tells him the full title of the painting is 'Gallifrey Falls No More'. The homeworld of the Time Lords is out there, somewhere. The Doctor is going home. He's just taking the long way around.

Trivia and facts

Showrunner Steven Moffat's original idea was to bring all three 'modern' Doctors together for the anniversary special, with Christopher Eccleston, David Tennant and Matt Smith all taking centre stage. Early drafts of the script featured the Ninth Doctor, as played by Eccleston and Moffat met with the actor to discuss his involvement with the anniversary special, but he turned it down.

Speaking at the Rose City Comic Con in September 2019, Eccleston explained to the convention why he took that action:

I didn't feel that what they were asking me to do did justice to the Ninth Doctor. I liked Steven Moffat a lot. I considered it. But it had an enormous emotional impact on me, what happened with *Doctor Who*.

The first complete draft script of 'The Day of the Doctor' was dated 28 February 2013 and featured a reference to the two 1960s Doctor Who movies, which are not considered part of the show's official canon. In one scene, which was never filmed, Clare spotted an image in the Black Archive, and Kate Stewart explained it was the actor Peter Cushing, who starred in the films as Doctor Who.

In order to differentiate between the different incarnations of the Time Lord, stage directions referred to them as 'The Eleventh Doctor', 'The Tenth Doctor' and 'The Other Doctor'. The first day of shooting for the anniversary special was 28 March 2013 on the Tardis set. The Trafalgar Square scenes were shot on 9 April, with Matt Smith hoisted over 90 metres in the air and hanging on a wire under the Tardis.

Tom Baker's appearance as the Curator was filmed on 26 April, which was also Matt Smith's final day filming. In order to keep his role secret, the production team decided that rather than have him stay overnight in a hotel in Cardiff, he would be collected from his East Sussex home at 1.30 am and driven to Cardiff to film his scenes that morning and then driven back later in the day.

The very last piece of the anniversary special to be filmed was Peter Capaldi's surprise appearance, which was recorded in strict secrecy on the set on 3 October 2013, which was the same day the Twelfth Doctor filmed the regeneration sequence for the upcoming Christmas special that would see the departure of Matt Smith.

Animations

Introduction

Such was the rock star status of the Tenth Doctor that it was only a matter of time before the BBC unleashed a multitude of spinoffs to meet the almost insatiable demand among fans for more content.

Alongside the action figures, audiobooks and spinoffs, like the *Sarah Jane Adventures* and *Torchwood,* the BBC also commissioned two animated series, which were aimed at slightly younger audiences. This was not entirely new territory for the programme. Three animated stories had been produced for the BBC's official Doctor Who website –'Scream of the Shalka', 'Shada' and 'Death Comes to Time' - before Russell T. Davies rebooted the series. But it was the first time an animated series had been broadcast alongside the regular episodes.

The first of these new animations was 'The Infinite Quest', which starred both David Tennant and Freema Agyeman and was set at some point during the third series. It was originally broadcast in three-minute segments during part of the children's television show *Totally Doctor Who*. It was later edited into a 45-minute long omnibus edition, which has since been released on DVD and Blu-Ray.

The second animated series was entitled 'Dreamland', with just starred David Tennant and was initially shown on the BBC's Red Button service and Iplayer in the UK, before later being broadcast on BBC2 and BBC HD. 'Dreamland' was originally six episodes long, before a 42-minute omnibus edition was later released.

'The Infinite Quest'

Original UK airdate: 2 April to 30 June 2007 (individual episodes) and 30 June 2007 as a full story
Cast: David Tennant as The Doctor, Freema Agyeman as Martha Jones, Anthony Head as Baltazar, Toby Longworth as Caw/Squawk, Liza Tarbuck as Captain Kaliko, Tom Farrelly as Swabb, Lizzie Hopley as the Mantasphid Queen, Paul Clayton as Mergrass, Steven Meo as Pilot Kevin, Barney Harwood as Control Voice, Stephen Grief as Gurney and Dan Morgan as Locke/Warders
Written by Alan Barnes
Directed by Gary Russell
Music by Murray Gold
Produced by James Goss and Ros Attille
Filming dates: Running time: 45 minutes

Review

The idea of sending the Doctor and his companion on a quest to find a number of objects, probably seemed like a good idea at the time. After all, the concept is not exactly new, having been the basis for an entire series in the Fourth Doctor era as the Time Lord searched for the Key to Time.

But despite walking a well-worn path, 'The Infinite Quest' still manages to be an unsatisfying experience, possibly because it was originally broadcast in three-minute chunks, which mean the story moves along far too quickly. Characters and planets come and go, and even the 45-minute omnibus edition feels rushed. The anime-style figures, particularly the Doctor himself, never really convince. At least Antony Head seems to be enjoying himself as Baltazar, but if you're going to watch just one of the Tenth Doctor animations, you should pick 'Dreamland', which is far superior.

The Story

The Doctor and Martha Jones encounter an evil alien, called Baltazar, who is searching for four data chips to unlock an ancient spaceship, The Infinite, which can grant people their heart desires.

Sometime after defeating Baltazar, the Doctor and Martha meet his metal bird, Caw. The metal bird gives them the first data chip and tells them that each chip will lead to the next one. The Doctor and Martha start hunting for the next chip and end up on the planet Boukan, where the pirate Captain Kaliko is raiding the living oil rigs they find there. After Captain Kaliko is murdered, the Doctor and Martha take her data chip and set off to find the next one.

They discover the next chip on the planet Myarr, where it is being used as a necklace by a lizard alien named Mergrass. The final data chip is on the ice prison planet Volag-Noc. However, as soon as they have arrived, the Doctor is identified as a wanted criminal and imprisoned with a damaged android. Baltazar and Caw arrive on the ice prison planet after the last data chip is discovered. The villain marches the Doctor and Martha back into the Tardis and uses its equipment to find the final location of The Infinite. With the course set, Baltazar leaves the Doctor on the ice planet and sets off in the Tardis with Martha.

Baltazar sends Martha inside the spaceship to investigate. The Doctor arrives and then the ship states to fall apart. The Tardis departs, leaving Baltazar to rely on another robot bird, called Sqawk, who takes him back to Volag-Noc, where he is imprisoned.

Trivia

Set at some point during the third series of Doctor Who.'The Infinite Quest' was animated by the Manchester-based company Firestep, with another local company, Kilogramme, providing the computer-generated imagery.

Speaking to the Manchester Evening News in August 2007, one of Firestep's managing directors, Steve Maher, said it is an honour to be associated with the BBC's most successful programme:

> It has been very important for us to maintain the feel of the live-action series while making the most of the possibilities afforded by animations.
> Russell T. Davies - who writes the Doctor Who television series - has overseen the script for this and we've also liaised closely with the team in Cardiff, who film the programmes. It has also been an honour to help create new baddies, like Baltazar, for Doctor Who to face.

While Christian Johnson, creative director of Kilogramme, said in the same article:

> Many of the animators who have worked on 'Infinite Quest' - including myself and Steve Maher - used to work for Cosgrove Hall productions and so have a wealth of talent between us.
>
> A lot of computer-generated imagery is now farmed out to large studios overseas, so we're really happy that this show is being produced in the North West.

'Dreamland'

Original UK airdate: 21-26 November 2009 (episodes) and 5 December 2009 (full story)
Cast: David Tennant as The Doctor, Georgia Tennant as Cassie Rice, Tim Howar as Jimmy Stalkingwolf, Lisa Bowerman as SarubaVelak, David Warner as Lord Azlok, Stuart Milligan as Colonel Stark, Clarke Peters as Night Eagle, Nicholas Rowe as Rivesh Mantilax, Peter Guiness as Mister Dread and Ryan McCluskey as Soldiers
Written by Phil Ford
Directed by Gary Russell
Music by Murray Gold
Produced by Ed Cross and Mat Fidell
Running time: 42 minutes

Review

Wearing its 1950s science fiction influences firmly on its sleeves, Dreamland is a frequently overlooked gem in the Tenth Doctor canon. Admittedly, the animation might not be up the standards of a multi-milliondollar Pixar film, but it fits the script's b-movie feel perfectly. The Viperox aliens and the Men in Black are particularly good.

Writer Phil Ford delivers a fastpaced and action-packed story, which rattles along with plenty of good lines for all the cast to enjoy. The script even contains a few cheeky nods to classic movies, like *Star Wars* and *Independence Day*. There's even a *Die Hard* reference. Something for the dads, as they used to say.

In some ways, it's a shame 'Dreamland' could not have been filmed as one of the 'Specials', as it feels like a bona fide Doctor Who adventure that deserves a much bigger audience. Mind you, even the television programme's production team might have struggled to find a location in South Wales to double for the Nevada desert. Maybe, some things are best left to the animators.

The Story

The Tardis lands near a diner in Dry Springs, Nevada in 1958, where the Doctor meets a young waitress, Cassie Rice and a native American, Jimmy Stalkingwolf. The Time Lord spots an alien artefact on the diner counter. But seconds after he activates it, two Men in Black appear. Jimmy tells the Doctor he has seen a 'space monster' eating cattle on a nearby ranch. They decide to investigate and discover a large alien creature, called a Viperox battle drone.

Before the alien can attack, it is destroyed by American soldiers, who take the Doctor and his companions to a secret military base, Area 51 or Dreamland as it is sometimes known. After escaping from a locked room, they find a spaceship in a hangar and use it to escape. After being pursued by jet fighters, the Doctor has to crash land the ship near an abandoned mining town, called Solitude. In an underground mine, they discover a Viperox Queen, who is busy laying eggs.

After escaping from the mine, they meet Jimmy's grandfather Night Eagle, who takes the Doctor to meet another alien, Rivesh Mantilax, who crashed in the desert five years ago. Rivesh came to Earth searching for his wife, who the Doctor believes is the alien they saw in Area 51. But their conversation is interrupted by Colonel Stark and his soldiers, who bring them all back to the military base. They realise Colonel Stark is working with the Viperox. The Doctor convinces Stark not to trust the Viperox, but their leader, Lord Azlok becomes angry and escapes.

A swarm of Viperox soldiers attack Area 51, but the Doctor is able to use a biological weapon developed by Rivesh to force the alien soldiers to retreat and leave Earth for good.

Trivia and facts

The animation for Dreamland was commissioned by BBC Drama Multiplatform and produced by the Brighton-based company Littleloud.

The cast included Georgia Tennant, who of course, is married to David Tennant and is the daughter of the Fifth Doctor, Peter Davison. Another member of the cast was Lisa Bowerman, who has several claims to fame as far as Doctor Who is concerned. Bowerman played Karra in Survival, which was the last story of the original run for the programme back in 1989. In addition, since 1998, she has played the archaeologist Bernice Summerfield in various Big Finish audio adventures.

In several of these Big adventures, she also appears alongside David Warner, who plays Lord Azlok in Dreamland and is an alternative 'unbound' version of the Doctor.

Above: David Tennant starts his tenure as The Doctor with 'The Christmas Invasion'. *(BBC)*

Below: The Doctor's first companion in the Tennant era, Billie Piper as Rose Tyler. *(BBC)*

Above: The second companion, Freema Agyeman as Martha Jones. *(BBC)*

Below: The third companion, Catherine Tate as Donna Noble. *(BBC)*

Above: An early appearance from Karen Gillan – later to star as Amy Pond during the Matt Smith era – here as a soothsayer in the 'Fires Of Pompeii'. *(BBC)*

Below: Another prophetic appearance – this time from future Doctor Peter Capaldi – also from the 'Fires Of Pompeii'. *(BBC)*

Above: Fenella Woolgar as Agatha Christie in 'The Unicorn and the Wasp'. (*BBC*)

Below: Steve Pemberton guests in 'Silence In The Library'. (*BBC*)

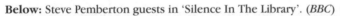

Above: Former companion and star of *The Sarah Jane Adventures,* the late Elizabeth Sladen, with her screen son Luke (Thomas Knight) in 'Journey's End'. (*BBC*)

Below: The *Torchwood* cast: John Barrowman, Eve Myles and Gareth David-Lloyd in 'Journey's End'. (*BBC*)

Above: Timothy Dalton as Time Lord President Rassilon in 'The End Of Time'. (*BBC*)

Below: Matt Smith, David Tennant and The War Doctor (the late John Hurt) in the terrific 'Day Of The Doctor'. (*BBC*)

On Track series

Queen – Andrew Wild 978-1-78952-003-3

Emerson Lake and Palmer – Mike Goode 978-1-78952-000-2

Deep Purple and Rainbow 1968-79 – Steve Pilkington 978-1-78952-002-6

Yes – Stephen Lambe 978-1-78952-001-9

Blue Oyster Cult – Jacob Holm-Lupo 978-1-78952-007-1

The Beatles – Andrew Wild 978-1-78952-009-5

Roy Wood and the Move – James R Turner 978-1-78952-008-8

Genesis – Stuart MacFarlane 978-1-78952-005-7

JethroTull – Jordan Blum 978-1-78952-016-3

The Rolling Stones 1963-80 – Steve Pilkington 978-1-78952-017-0

Judas Priest – John Tucker 978-1-78952-018-7

Toto – Jacob Holm-Lupo 978-1-78952-019-4

Van Der Graaf Generator – Dan Coffey 978-1-78952-031-6

Frank Zappa 1966 to 1979 – Eric Benac 978-1-78952-033-0

Elton John in the 1970s – Peter Kearns 978-1-78952-034-7

The Moody Blues – Geoffrey Feakes 978-1-78952-042-2

The Beatles Solo 1969-1980 – Andrew Wild 978-1-78952-030-9

Steely Dan – Jez Rowden 978-1-78952-043-9

Hawkwind – Duncan Harris 978-1-78952-052-1

Fairport Convention – Kevan Furbank 978-1-78952-051-4

Iron Maiden – Steve Pilkington 978-1-78952-061-3

Dream Theater – Jordan Blum 978-1-78952-050-7

10CC – Peter Kearns 978-1-78952-054-5

Gentle Giant – Gary Steel 978-1-78952-058-3

Kansas – Kevin Cummings 978-1-78952-057-6

Mike Oldfield – Ryan Yard 978-1-78952-060-6

The Who – Geoffrey Feakes 978-1-78952-076-7

On Screen series
Carry On... – Stephen Lambe 978-1-78952-004-0

Powell and Pressburger – Sam Proctor 978-1-78952-013-2

Seinfeld Seasons 1 to 5 – Stephen Lambe 978-1-78952-012-5

Francis Ford Coppola – Cam Cobb and Stephen Lambe 978-1-78952-022-4

Monty Python – Steve Pilkington 978-1-78952-047-7

Doctor Who: The David Tennant Years – Jamie Hailstone 978-1-78952-066-8

James Bond – Andrew Wild 978-1-78952-010-1

Other Books
Not As Good As The Book – Andy Tillison 978-1-78952-021-7

The Voice. Frank Sinatra in the 1940s – Stephen Lambe 978-1-78952-032-3

Maximum Darkness – Deke Leonard 978-1-78952-048-4

The Twang Dynasty – Deke Leonard 978-1-78952-049-1

Maybe I Should've Stayed In Bed – Deke Leonard 978-1-78952-053-8

Tommy Bolin: In and Out of Deep Purple – Laura Shenton 978-1-78952-070-5

Jon Anderson and the Warriors - the road to Yes – David Watkinson
978-1-78952-059-0

and many more to come!

Would you like to write for Sonicbond Publishing?

At Sonicbond Publishing we are always on the look-out for authors, particularly for our two main series:

On Track. Mixing fact with in depth analysis, the On Track series examines the work of a particular musical artist or group. All genres are considered from easy listening and jazz to 60s soul to 90s pop, via rock and metal.

On Screen. This series looks at the world of film and television. Subjects considered include directors, actors and writers, as well as entire television and film series. As with the On Track series, we balance fact with analysis.

While professional writing experience would, of course, be an advantage the most important qualification is to have real enthusiasm and knowledge of your subject. First-time authors are welcomed, but the ability to write well in English is essential.

Sonicbond Publishing has distribution throughout Europe and North America, and all books are also published in E-book form. Authors will be paid a royalty based on sales of their book.

Further details are available from www.sonicbondpublishing.co.uk. To contact us, complete the contact form there or email info@sonicbondpublishing.co.uk